Worms Head

A POCKET GUIDE TO GOWER

THE GOWER SOCIETY
CYFEILLION GŴYR

'A Guide to Gower' was first published in 1965
by the Publications Committee of the Gower Society
which then consisted of
Evan Evans, Bernard Morris, T. R. Owen and J. Mansel Thomas (editor).

1st edition	1965
2nd edition	1966
3rd edition	1973
4th edition	1979
5th edition	1982
6th edition	1999
7th edition	2019

The editors gratefully acknowledge the work of their predecessors
and wish to thank all the authors of the articles, which have been fully revised

ISBN 978-0-902767-56-0

Published by
The Gower Society
c/o The Community Centre,
Victoria Road, Penclawdd, Swansea. SA4 3FU

Design by Peter Banks
This book is typeset in Perpetua and Gill Sans
Printed by
Gomer Press Limited, Llandysul, Ceredigion SA44 4JL

CONTENTS

ACKNOWLEDGEMENTS

This 7th Edition of the Guide to Gower, now *A Pocket Guide to Gower*, was compiled by the Publications Committee of the Gower Society. Members of the Committee are Rod Cooper (Chair), Peter Douglas-Jones, Andrew Dulley, Margaret ap Gwent, Charles Hill, Hildegarde Roberts, Sarah Samuel and Jane Sherrard-Smith. The Chair of the Committee wishes to acknowledge the dedication and hard work of its members over the two years that this work has taken. Particular thanks are due to Andrew Dulley for his work in designing the cover and producing maps for the new Guide. We also give thanks for the final checking and reading by Ruth and Malcolm Ridge. Many others have freely contributed to this guide and we are very grateful for this. Members of the Committee wish to acknowledge the debt owed to compilers of previous editions which continue to form the principal content of the Guide. In all, it is an expression of the commitment of local people to the recognition and conservation of this remarkable piece of land.

The photographs are, except where indicated otherwise, the work of the Gower Society's official photographer Peter Douglas-Jones.

We are indebted to Snake River Press Books in Sussex (www.snakeriverpress.co.uk) for allowing us to adopt their typography and styling for our new *Pocket Guide to Gower.*

INTRODUCTION

Welcome . . .

Come to Gower, and you will find your attention drawn by all sorts of things. There are prehistoric chambered tombs and standing stones to intrigue and fascinate, lanes that wind through little villages with their cottages and ancient churches, while craggy castle battlements and quiet little byways hint at ancient places long forgotten. There is inspiration to be found in breath-taking scenery, forever changing as the seasons turn. This guide will help you find your way around. There is a gazetteer of places of interest, accompanied by a series of articles on specific aspects of Gower's heritage and ecology.

So what is Gower? Most people think of it as the peninsula to the west of Swansea, where the first Area of Outstanding Natural Beauty was designated in 1956. It is also a parliamentary constituency and an archdeaconry of the Church in Wales, and all of them have different boundaries. Over the years it has been many things, and this guide aims to take account of them all.

Gower had the dubious honour of being on the western frontier of Norman Wales. Before the conquest it had been part of the Welsh Deheubarth, but shortly after 1100 it was taken over by Henry de Beaumont and his Norman knights. Thereupon it became the marcher lordship of Gower and Kilvey, one of a string of such territories stretching along the south and east of Wales. Each one operated like a separate country. Its marcher lord was all-powerful in his domain, but owed allegiance to the English crown. Thus the lordship of Gower was its own little realm, set between lands of the Welsh princes to the west and the rest of Norman-controlled Wales to the east. It was much more than just the peninsula, which made up about half its total area. At its heart were the two boroughs of Swansea and Loughor, and it stretched northwards from there almost as far as Ammanford. In today's terms, it is the City and County of Swansea, with the addition of Pontardawe and district, and this is the area covered by this guide.

The Lordship of Gower is a land of contrasts, shaped by its geology, as explained in the chapter on landscape. The northern part is characterised by poorer soils and upland grazing, interspersed with rich coal veins. The southern part is better for agriculture and it is probable that this was historically where most people lived. As described in the sections on churches, chapels and crosses, this is where you will find most of the ancient churches, many of which predate the coming of the Normans. Soon after the Conquest this more fertile land was divided into manors which were given to Norman lords in exchange for military service. They built castles, many of which you can still visit. Today their ruins are peaceful, but they remind us that this area was once heavily-defended frontier country. The ones in Gower are all different, a mixture of styles and construction techniques, and the chapter on castles tells you all about them.

The manorial lords encouraged English settlers to become their tenants to help defend the land. South Gower has some villages with very English-sounding names: Nicholaston, Newton, Oxwich, Horton, Knelston, and so on, and for good reason; Isaac Hamon, writing in 1697, tells us that in his day English was spoken over most of peninsular Gower, but with an accent and vocabulary all of its own. This Gower dialect, for centuries the standard speech of most of the peninsula, can no longer be heard except in an occasional intonation or turn of phrase, but the chapter on dialect gives a taste of what it was like.

Meanwhile, the north-eastern part of the peninsula, as well as most of the area to the north of Swansea, is poorer agricultural land. The Norman lords had no designs on that, but were content to let their Welsh tenants live much as they had always done. There, Welsh land law held sway and the Welsh language continued to flourish. Up in the north are large mountain commons, while others straddle the peninsula or skirt the coast. In fact, as the following chapter explains, Gower's commons are disproportionately large and are an important part of its heritage and ecology. They support a diversity of wildlife, something that continues out into the farmland, byways, woods and coasts. In-depth sections on each aspect of Gower's wildlife, including flowers, animals, birds, invertebrates and marine life, tell you what to look out for and help to explain the complexity of the fragile ecosystem.

The growth of smelting industries and the exploitation of coal led to the industrialisation of the South Wales valleys and the Swansea Valley was as badly affected as any. The scars of industry may have faded, but the legacy remains in the towns and villages of today. On the Gower peninsula, Penclawdd had a copper works and there were some collieries too, but little else. Overall, agriculture has had the greatest influence on the landscape, but here there have been profound changes, as the section on the rural economy explains. Once typified by small, mixed farms, agriculture is now more mainstream and profit-led. That said, the challenges of farming in today's world have driven many farmers to diversify, so while traditional small farms have given way to wheat and grazing, we now have archery, Christmas tree plantations and wedding venues alongside.

So this is Gower, a unique and beautiful place, shaped by its landscape and defined by its history. It is a place of variety and contrast, whose beauty is fragile; for those very things that attract and charm the visitor are under constant threat from careless use and poor management. The Gower Society has been in existence since 1948 and, briefly put, our aims are to encourage an appreciation of Gower and to safeguard all that makes it unique and special. These are our aims in presenting this guide, and we hope the reader will appreciate and enjoy it too.

About this edition

A Guide to Gower was first produced back in 1965 and has gone through several editions since then. In this, the seventh edition, it has gone back to its roots and become a hardback pocket guide once more. While articles have been rewritten and maps redrawn, we have retained the structure and many of the original features from the earlier editions. Among these are the charming line drawings in the gazetteer section, which were drawn by Alfred J. Lavender in the 1960s. Originally from Tyneside, he was appointed head of art at Swansea Grammar School (later Bishop Gore School) in the 1920s, staying there until his retirement in 1965. He was also honorary secretary of the Swansea Art Society.

We are indebted to all the people who worked hard to bring the Guide to fruition, including those who have contributed articles, artistry and expertise.

Parkmill

Abbreviations used in the Gazetteer

Cadw	Welsh Government's historic environment service
CP	Car park
E	East
FP	Footpath
Fr	French
ft	feet
GR	National Grid reference
HW	High water
HWM	High water mark
m	metre
N	North
NHM	Natural History Museum, London
NMW	National Museum of Wales, Cardiff
NWM	National Waterfront Museum, Swansea
NT	National Trust property
OE	Old English (linguistic)
PH	Public house
PO	Post office
S	South
Scand	Scandinavian (linguistic)
SSSI	Site of Special Scientific Interest
SM	Swansea Museum
W	West
WWII	World War Two
yds	yards

Words printed in italics are to suggest a helpful cross-reference within the gazetteer.

Stone stile at Llanrhidian church yard

Prince's fountain, Mumbles

GAZETTEER

ABER-LOGIN Originally a solitary farm on the *Loughor Estuary* to the W of *Wernffrwd*. First recorded in the seventeenth century, the name is the only instance on the Ordnance Survey map of Gower of the Welsh 'aber', which carries the meaning estuary and can also refer to the mouth of a river or the confluence of two streams. 'Login' derives from Welsh 'halog' (note *Wern Halog* nearby) meaning dirty or muddy, and the name could be a reference to a muddy stream. **SS511938**

ARTHUR'S STONE Remarkable dolmen on *Cefn Bryn*. A Neolithic chambered tomb (about 2500 BC), constructed of stone of uncertain origin. Capstone said to weigh over 25 tons. Frost, lightning, a miller in search of a millstone and King Arthur's sword have all been blamed for the split-off portion. The stone is possibly the Maen Ceti, one of the wonders of the ancient Isle of Britain. One legend tells that it was a pebble shed from King Arthur's shoe and another that Arthur's Stone goes down to the sea to drink on New Year's Eve. ½ mile SE is a holy well, formerly part of the Gower water supply. Small cairns are scattered over the hilltop.

Reached by FP, N from highest point of road crossing Cefn Bryn from *Cillibion* to *Reynoldston*. **SS491906**

BACKINGSTONE Iron Age promontory fort located on a spur on the E edge of *Bishopston Valley* 1 mile SW of Bishopston.

Backingstone Chapel, thirteenth century, dedicated to St Peter, functioned as a private oratory. Now a ruin in a field, left of the FP to Bishopston Valley from *Pyle Corner*.

SS568877 and SS576881

BACON HOLE One of Gower's largest and best known bone caves at *Deepslade* (Hunts Bay) with over a 20 m (66 ft) wide entry. It extends for 45 m (148 ft) into the cliff W of *Pwlldu Head*. Ancient bones, including narrow-nosed rhinoceros and straight-tusked elephant, were discovered around 1850 by Colonel Wood. It was here in 1912 that the 10 wide red colour bands were discovered, giving the cave its name. It was later agreed that the colour variation was due to the red oxide mineral seeping through the rock. Access is restricted at various times of the year due to breeding birds and hibernating bats. **SS563868**

BANTAM BAY Secluded cove and beach used by smugglers and for the export of limestone. Located E of *Pwlldu Head* and site of Ring Rock. See also *Pwlldu*. **SS575866**

BARLAND CASTLE (on private land) See *Bishopston Old Castle*.

BARLAND COMMON Open Millstone Grit moorland alongside main road directly N of *Bishopston Valley*. Limestone quarrying near here has uncovered a few small stalactite caverns, with some prehistoric remains now in SM. Stream disappears underground near N edge of quarry. **SS578897**

BEGGARS PIT near *Penrice*. Large sink hole, one of a series, adjacent to public FP, S of *Hangman's Cross*. Unfortunately, there is no evidence to support the theory that it was a burial site for plague victims and/or corpses from the gibbet at Hangman's Cross. **SS481866**

BENRICK See *Great Tor*.

BERGES ISLAND NE tip of *Whiteford Burrows* and a popular location for bird watchers. Once one of Gower's four tidal islands, the others being *Mumbles Head*, *Worms Head* and *Burry Holms*. **SS448957**

BERTHLWYD PH and restaurant (currently The

Rake and Riddle), farms and domestic buildings between *Gowerton* and *Penclawdd*. Formerly the site of coal mines dating back to Tudor times. The largest of the mines was *Wernbwll*. At Berthlwyd Uchaf, a nearby farm, traces of a small eighteenth-century pottery have been found. Details of the pottery can be found at SM. During WWII, Berthlwyd was a pivotal part of an army firing range that extended across the entire length of the marshes and sands of the *Burry Estuary*.

SS566964

BERRY Name given to small collection of farms near Scurlage. Ringwork (traces only) ½ mile NE; the Wildlife Trust of South and West Wales reserve is nearby in Berry Wood.

SS472878

BETLANDS Farm on *Burry Pill* 1 mile NW of *Llanddewi*.

SS455896

BISHOPSTON (Welsh – Llandeilo Ferwallt). Large village at head of *Bishopston Valley* formerly a centre for market gardening. Now a number of private housing developments surround the old village. PO, 2 PHs, shops. The former Providence (English Congregational) chapel, built in 1807, is a Guide activity centre. The Joiners' Arms brews local ales in its own brew house. The original Malt House, on Bishopston Road, has been converted into a dwelling.

The church, St Teilo's, located in the valley below the present village centre, is one of Gower's medieval buildings. The parish of Bishopston had within its bounds Llans (church communities) which date back to the earliest days of the Celtic Church (late fifth-sixth century). The parish is identified in grants recorded in the Book of Llandaff. In the days of the Celtic Church, it may have been a minor mother church attached to the great mother church at Llandaff, and remained part of the diocese of Llandaff until the rationalisation of diocesan boundaries in 1847. The present building probably grew out of an earlier chapel and took on its present extent during the thirteenth century. Within the chancel is an early piscina and the present font, thirteenth century, seems to be standing on one of an even earlier period. On the S side of the church are the remains of a medieval churchyard cross (possibly fourteenth century). The parish contained sanctuary land in medieval times adjacent to *Backingstone* Chapel above Bishopston Valley.

Iron Age promontory fort at Backingstone (1 mile SW).

Nearest Bays: *Caswell* (2 miles by road); *Brandy Cove* (½ mile), *Pwlldu* (1½ miles) accessible by paths only, from *Pyle Corner*.

BISHOPSTON OLD CASTLE also known as Barland Castle. Early Norman ringwork timber castle on N edge of *Barland Common*, overlooking the delightful *Bishopston Valley* and stream. Incorrectly called a 'motte' on the OS mapping. Probably a rare episcopal castle, built within the only property in Gower that was retained by the Bishopric of Llandaff after a dispute with St David's in the time of Bishop Urban (1107-34). Noteworthy as one of the earliest archæologically excavated and published (by Colonel William Llewelyn Morgan in 1898) Norman timber castles in the UK. Site is overgrown and in private ownership. **SS582900**

BISHOPSTON VALLEY (NT) accessible by FPs only, not all of them easy going. Rugged wooded valley of the Bishopston stream, winding 2½ miles from near Bishopston Church to *Pwlldu Bay*. Of considerable botanical and geological interest. There are various limestone sinkholes, the largest of which is known as the Daw Pit. The stream is partly subterranean, in wet weather flowing above ground much of the way; in dry weather it can be heard flowing underground, notably at *Guzzlehole*, halfway down the valley. The bed of the stream opposite St Teilo's Church is known as The Creten (Latin – *cretena*, a torrent) corrupted and known locally as The Gritten. Guzzlehole is opposite remains of Long Ash Lead Mine in valley.

Access on foot from the side road opposite *Barland Common, Kittle Green, Widegate* (lane opp Pennard Church), *Pyle Corner*, or entirely by FP from *Pwlldu Bay*. **SS587903 – SS574872**

BISHOP'S WOOD See *Caswell Valley*.

BLACKPILL Village suburb of Swansea on the edge of the sea, midway between Swansea and *Mumbles*. Blackpill Lido with children's playground and a café in the former electrical sub-station (designed by Ernest Morgan) on the Mumbles Railway. 'Roman Bridge' on Clyne River probably eighteenth century restored. Swansea Bay cycle-path and FP skirts the edge of the Lido, following the line of the Mumbles Railway. PH and restaurant The Woodman, small local shop and petrol station.

See *Clyne Castle, Clyne Valley*.
SS619905

Roman bridge, Blackpill

BLUE ANCHOR Community in NE Gower on the hill above *Penclawdd*. The name derives from a former PH built here on the original turnpike road leading from *Penclawdd* to *Three Crosses* and possibly dating from the construction of that road in the late eighteenth century.
SS552951

BLUEPOOL CORNER (also known as Bluepool Bay) Sandy cove when tide out; accessible on foot only; FP across dunes from *Llangennith* (2 miles) or from *Burry Holms* at the N tip of *Rhossili Bay*. The Blue Pool is a circular rock pool 5 m across, once thought to be bottomless. Numbers of gold doubloons and moidores were found near here. Fine natural archway W of the bay, known as Three Chimneys. In sand dunes nearby remains of a stone-walled Iron Age enclosure. Two small caves near here. The cave in the cliff to the W is known as Culver Hole, see entry for *Culver Hole (2)* not to be confused with Culver Hole *(1)* near *Port Eynon*. To the E is a small sea cavern of no special importance known as Cathole, not to be confused with Cathole in Green Cwm. **SS409930**

BOVEHILL CASTLE also known as Landimore Castle. The ruins are of a short-lived, later medieval castle or fortified manorial complex, visible from the lane to the marshes.

Probably built by Sir Hugh Johnys in the late fifteenth century and abandoned in the early Tudor period. Sir Hugh, Crusader and once Knight Marshall of England, is reputed to have supplied the castle well with water conveyed through lead pipes. It has been claimed that pipe sections have been found in a field on the W side of the castle. A well ½ mile SW of the castle is named Leaden Pipe Well. Castle is in private ownership. **SS465933**

BRACELET BAY (derived from Broad Slade) The first of the limestone bays of Gower, after leaving Swansea Bay and rounding *Mumbles Head*. Pebbly, some sand, rock pools. A fine example of a fossil coral reef can be seen in the middle portion of the bay (just below the rim path). To W is *Tutt Hill*, with former coastguard station and major maritime rescue co-ordination centre (closed 2015), then *Limeslade Bay*. Walks up *Mumbles Hill* and along coast. CPs, restaurant. Lifeguards on hand May-September. Seasonal dog ban 1st May-30th September. **SS631872**

BRANDY COVE Little inlet ½ mile W of *Caswell*. Once known as Hareslade Cove, became known as Brandy Cove in nineteenth century because of its association with smuggling. Excellent exposures of the Pleistocene raised beach, marking a time when sea level was about 9 m (30 ft) higher than today. FP through wooded slade/valley (*Hareslade*) from *Pyle Corner* (1 mile). Lead mines once worked here. FP from *Caswell* (¼ mile E), *Pwlldu* (1 mile W). **SS586874**

BROAD POOL Small stretch of fresh water alongside main road crossing *Cefn Bryn* from north road (B4271) at *Cillibion*. Permanent nature reserve, rich in water plants (including the rare yellow fringed water-lily), insect and bird-life (duck, heron, swan, grebe etc). Water held up through subsidence of glacial boulder clay into dissolved caverns in the underlying limestone. See also *Moormills*. **SS510910**

BROUGHTON BAY (pronounced bruffton). Broad, sandy, dune-fringed bay 1 mile N of *Llangennith*, facing NW. Access by lane from village, then FP. Estuary tides here make bathing dangerous. In 1868 sixteen vessels outward bound from Llanelli were wrecked on the same tide. Marks N emergence of the important geological fault that defines the W side of *Rhossili Down*. FPs to *Bluepool Corner* (1 mile W) and to *Whiteford Burrows* (1½ miles E) **SS420932**

BRYN-SIL Farm ruin on bridleway to *Berry*, N of *Hangman's Cross*. **SS482871**

BULWARK, THE A large defended enclosure of Iron Age date prominently sited at the E end of *Llanmadoc Hill*. The surrounding banks and ditches are well preserved and are complex in plan. Their form suggests that the original defences were progressively enlarged. **SS443928**

BURRY Hamlet of small farmhouses with characteristic narrow Gower lane. Burry Lane connects *Llanddewi* to *Burry Green* and *Llangennith*, and runs parallel with *Burry Pill*, the nearest Gower has to a river. **SS458904**

BURRY ESTUARY See *Loughor, River.*

BURRY GREEN Pretty hamlet on road to *Llangennith*. The Methodist Bethesda chapel is the earliest chapel in peninsular Gower still holding meetings every Sunday. Built in 1813, it was the first of six Gower chapels founded by Lady Barham, who financially supported the 'Apostle of Gower', William Griffith. A memorial to Griffith can be found in the chapel. Lady Barham's son, the Earl of Gainsborough, conveyed the chapel to the Calvinistic Methodists (now known as the Presbyterian Church of Wales) in 1855. Unusually, the access to the rear and side balcony, the latter bowed, is by an external stone staircase at the rear of the building. FPs, S to Burry and N across *Ryer's Down*. See also *Cadiz Hall.* **SS462914**

BURRY HOLMS (holm – Old Scandinavian for island) Small limestone tidal island at N tip of *Rhossili Bay*. 9000 years ago Burry Holms was an inland, tree-covered hill. Charcoal remains and hunting tools are evidence that there was once a

Mesolithic settlement here. An Iron Age earthwork consisting of a single bank and ditch bisects the island. Ruins of a medieval monastic settlement. The sixth century St Cenydd has strong associations with this area and the medieval ruins may represent a centre of pilgrimage connected with his memory. Access only at low tide.

See also *Spaniard Rocks*.
SS400925

BURRY INLET See *Loughor, River*.

Burry Middle Mill

BURRY PILL One of the major streams of Gower, which once provided water power for seven mills. Originating from springs below *Cefn Bryn*, it drains into *Loughor Estuary* near *Berges Island*. **SS450980**

See also *Burry*.

BURRY STONES See *Knelston*.

BUTTERSLADE (? from butte – blunt, rounded). See *Thurba Head*.

BUTTER WELL See *Llanrhidian*.

CADIZ HALL. Curiously named cottage on the lane south of Burry Green. This is not a reference to Cadiz or the Spanish Armada (as sometimes thought) but to the Cady or Cade family, established in Gower in the Middle Ages, who had a holding nearby. **SS465909**

CANNISLAND PARK Named after the field Cannisland and adjacent to Cannisland Wood in Ilston Valley. This unusual name very likely derives from St Cenydd, who is associated with Gower. It is recorded that there was a small oratory of St Cenydd near Trinity Well in Ilston Valley and there was glebe land nearby including Cannisland. The name seems not far removed from 'Cenydd's land'.

See *Kilvrough Manor*. **SS564901**

CARTERSFORD BRIDGE At a point on north road (B4271) where it dips and bends into a wooded valley to cross the small Ilston Stream. Marks boundary of *Fairwood Common* with *Pengwern Common*. Once the site of a smithy and the old turnpike gate. In 1844, the gatekeeper was killed in an incident with Christopher Batcock, the miller of Llanrhidian. **SS552914**

CASWELL BAY (possibly from Cresswell or cress stream). Believed to be the 'Porth Tulon' mentioned in a Papal Bull of 1128. Popular, easily accessible, but still one of the most picturesque of Gower bays. Sheltered by cliffs and a fringe of pine trees, firm sands, CPs, refreshments, shops, toilets, showers. A popular spot for surfers. Lifeguards during the summer; seasonal dog ban (1st May-30th September). The beach is advertised as being accessible for wheelchair users. Bishop's Wood Nature Reserve is in the valley at the far end of CP. Terminus for Swansea buses. The hymn-writer Frances Ridley Havergal (1836-1879), who wrote the hymn 'Take My Life and Let It Be', lived here briefly until her death. See *Newton*. Iron Age earthwork above W of the bay on Redley Cliff. FPs to *Langland* (1½ miles E), *Pwlldu* (1 mile W) via *Brandy Cove*.

CASWELL VALLEY is a short wooded valley with walks, entrance from CP opposite bay, to *Bishopston* (1½ miles N) and *Murton* (1 mile N). Bishop's Wood – rare ancient limestone woodland (SSSI), the site of a round-house run by the Countryside Centre and Forest School. Ruins of three buildings can be seen – a priest's cell, a chapel and a holy well dedicated to St Peter. It has been asserted that these buildings constituted the 'Porth Tulon' mentioned in the Book of Llandaff, a twelfth-century diocesan document and important source for the early history of Gower.

See also *Holt's Field* under *Manselfield*. **SS593876**

CATHAN Isolated group of three former farmhouses on SW slope of *Hardings Down*. **SS436902**

CATHOLE I (or Cat's Hole) An interesting inland bone-cave in Green Cwm, *Parkmill*, quite easily found. Follow lane from near Gower Heritage Centre in Parkmill for about a mile to CP and then through gate erected by the Ramblers' Association, suitable for disabled access, into valley; pass Neolithic tomb known as *Giant's Grave*, and 180 m (200 yds) further on, climb steep slope to the right. Cave about 15 m (50 ft) up. Access from north road (A4217) by FP starting at *Llethrid*. **SS537900**

CATHOLE 2 See *Bluepool Corner*.

CEFN BRYN (Welsh – ridge hill) Old Red Sandstone spine of the peninsula, running WNW. from *Penmaen* to *Burry Green* (over 4 miles). The second highest point in Gower, 188 m (617 ft), its slopes dominate almost every inland view. This is the best place to scan the whole face of Gower, with its changing light and colours and variety of landscape. In the foreground is an intricate field pattern of small well-kept farms, woods and moorland. Further S the fringe of limestone cliffs and sandy bays (notably *Oxwich* and *Three Cliffs*), and, to the N, salt marshes and the *Loughor Estuary*. In the distance, a vast expanse of the Bristol Channel with the granite Lundy Island (to SW); and the heights of Somerset (Exmoor), Devon (Hartland Point), Pembrokeshire (Preseli Hills), Breconshire (Beacons), Carmarthenshire (the Fans).

The main route for traffic across Cefn Bryn, formerly known as the Old Coal Road (or Red Road), is from the north road (B4271) at *Cillibion* towards *Reynoldston*.

A fine Green Way from *Penmaen* (behind the former workhouse which later became an old people's home, originally Glan y Môr and then Three Cliffs Nursing Home), runs the whole length of the Bryn and is a spectacular walk. It is known as Talbot's Road. C R M Talbot, a nineteenth-century owner of Penrice Castle, made good use of it for hunting and picnicking parties. A carriageway from Penrice meets it just above *Home Farm*.

The Gower Way crosses Cefn Bryn from Penmaen to Reynoldston on its way between *Penlle'r Castell* and *Rhossili*. *The Gower Way Stone* at the eastern end of the Bryn was unveiled by HRH the Prince of Wales in 1998 to inaugurate the Gower Way. Above Reynoldston, and near where the Red Road crosses the Bryn, is a viewpoint at which stands a direction finder installed by the local Round Table to commemorate the Silver Jubilee, in 1977, of Queen Elizabeth II. Cefn Bryn is on Cadw's Register of Landscape of Historic Interest in Wales. It contains a number of important prehistoric monuments including *Arthur's Stone,* a burial site of the first farmers on Gower. See also *Broad Pool*. **SS504895**

CHAPEL MERE Pond in fields N of *Horton*. Water was once carried on donkeys from here to supply the surrounding area. The origin of the name is obscure. **SS474868**

CHERITON (probably Church Village). Tiny village 1 mile E of *Llanmadoc*. The place name dates from about 1330, which is the approx date of the church. St Cadog's is one of the most beautiful of the Gower churches. Being within the manor of *Landimore* (a further mile E) there has long been speculation that the former church was in Landimore, but this cannot be confirmed from historical sources and seems, on balance, to be unlikely.

The church was built early fourteenth century and is widely regarded as the most elegant and distinguished of Gower's medieval buildings. In common with the Glebe House it was under the control of the Knights Hospitaller in Pembrokeshire. Between 1540 and 1923 the Lord Chancellor was responsible for it. The entrance is a fine example of a doorway from the Decorated period and within the chancel is a tub-shaped font of some antiquity. In the arch at the end of the nave can be seen the old rood loft entrance, which at one time could be approached up steps set in the wall of the choir. The bell dates from 1736.

The Glebe House, adjacent to the church, is fourteenth-century. Built for the Order of Knights Hospitaller (Knights of St John), it was once the rectory for the parish. It is the oldest inhabited building in Gower.

FPs up wooded valley to *Stembridge* (1½ miles SE). Over hill to *Llangennith* (2 miles SW). See also *North Hill Tor.*

SS451932

CILLIBION (an early form was Gelli-libion, wet woods) Where road crossing *Cefn Bryn* branches off north road 1½ miles E of Llanrhidian.

The fields from Cillibion S to Cefn Bryn once belonged to Neath Abbey. ½ mile W of road junction is a fine Bronze Age burial mound – *Pen-y-Crug*. FPs to *Welsh Moor, Parkmill*. See also *Moormills.* **SS516914**

CILIFOR TOP Prominent rounded hill of Millstone Grit ½ mile E of *Llanrhidian*. Site of large Iron Age hill fort/ earthwork occupying 8 acres, one of the most extensive in this area. In the SE corner of the prehistoric hill fort lie the earthwork remains of a twelfth-century Norman timber ringwork castle, which is strategically sited to dominate views to the E, S and W, rather than to the coast to N.

Cilifor Top is clearly seen from *Cefn Bryn*; there is access on foot from the B4295 N of the junction with B4271; also from the minor road over *Welsh Moor* west of Parc-y-rhedyn Farm.

SS507922

CLYNE CASTLE Built as Woodlands in 1791 and remodelled in the Gothic style in the early nineteenth century. Renamed Clyne Castle by the Vivian family, who owned the estate from the early Victorian period to 1952, when the Borough of Swansea acquired it. Swansea University had halls of residence here from 1955. In 2003 the castle was converted to luxury flats; and houses fill the garden behind the Castle. Surrounded by Clyne Gardens, holding part of the National Collections of Rhododendrons, Pieris and Enkianthus, many planted by Admiral Walker-Heneage-Vivian, the last owner. The Gardens are owned by Swansea Council and are open to the public. The wooded Brockhole Valley on the west side has a bog garden and many species of ornamental shrubs and trees; and the parkland on the E side rises to wonderful views across Swansea Bay. Just inside the entrance off St Catwg's Walk is the small pets' cemetery where Vivian pets were buried. Clyne Chapel was built in 1907 by Graham Vivian for his family's use. **SS615906**

CLYNE COMMON Approx 1 mile along the B4436 from its junction with Mumbles Road at *Blackpill*. Open, airy moorland (of millstone grit), with fine long views of Gower, Swansea Bay and Mumbles Head. Eighteen-hole golf course and many FPs. **SS595902**

CLYNE VALLEY *Clyne Castle* and Gardens lie at the S end of Clyne Valley. The Clyne Valley Country Park is Swansea's only country park. It lies along each side of the Clyne river and has a very varied habitat. A railway ran through the valley from 1867 until 1964. Built by the Llanelly Railway & Dock Co, it was taken over in 1873 by the London & North Western Railway and then in 1923 became part of the London, Midland & Scottish. Its route now provides the cycleway and FP through the valley. It links with the cycleway and FP around Swansea Bay, which also follows the former railway track. Cycle track 4 of the National Cycleway Network follows the route from Blackpill to Killay, Gowerton and Loughor. The Valley is a former industrial landscape with many marks of industry remaining including coal levels, traces of bell pits, small quarries, tramways and canals. The Ivy Tower was actually the smoke stack for the early nineteenth-century arsenic works. A brick works was present from the 1870s to the mid 1960s – a few traces include the bricks found in the paths through the woods. Some sites have Ancient Monument designation. Part of the Mumbles Railway, the first in the world to carry passengers, ran up the valley and was mainly used to bring coal and other goods from the valley to Swansea Docks. **SS610915**

COCKSTREET Characteristic Gower lane, leading from *Llangennith* to *Broughton Bay*. Recalls gaming and cock-fighting days of this once lawless part of the peninsula. The original farm off Cockstreet has been converted into a number of cottages. **SS426920**

COETY GREEN Small group of old and new dwellings SW of Llangennith where two streams meet. As Diles Lake, the stream reaches the sea across Rhossili sands. The water once turned wheels for three mills.
SS427910

COLD COMFORT See *Merrysun*.

COLLEGE MILL Site of an ancient mill dating from at least the thirteenth century.
SS427914

CRABART Part of the tidal Shipway between *Worms Head* and the mainland, especially those far-out flatter rocks forming a spit E towards *Tears Point* and exposed only at low tide. **SS401869**

CRAWLEY POINT See *Nicholaston*.

CRAWLEY WOODS (locally Crowley) See *Nicholaston*.

CRICKTON Farm near *Llanrhidian* on N edge of *Cefn Bryn* common. The name is thought to derive from the nearby Bronze Age round barrow, Pen-y-crug (Crug-ton). According to a local nineteenth-century diarist the name was pronounced 'Creekton' which would conform with this derivation. **SS504917**

CROFTY Original settlement dates from Tudor times. But this much changed village on the edge of the marshes of the *Loughor Estuary* began to grow around 1880 as a group of miners' cottages which still stand at the centre of the original village. Now the area, with its processing plant, has become the principal modern site of the N Gower cockle industry although harvesting of cockles is decreasing.

Zoar Presbyterian Church was built in the middle of Crofty in 1884. Crofty Inn was once a substantial farmhouse surrounded by a few small cottages or crofts from which the village derived its name.

Lane (impassable at high tide) along edge of salt marshes to *Llanrhidian* (2 miles W). **SS527951**

CROWDERS QUAY See *Port Eynon*.

CULVER HOLE 1. A most intriguing walled-in cave W of Port Eynon Point. Accessible at sea level, but only up to half tide, by tracks around the point and from cliff top, or from *Overton Mere* (immediately W). One of the mysteries of Gower is how this fantastic 18 m (60 ft) wall of masonry, pierced by look-out windows, came to be built in such a remote part of the coast. From the name (OE culfer: pigeon) it seems to have been used as a columbarium or dove-cote, where pigeons were bred for food, or perhaps a natural breeding-place for this bird; such holes may be seen above the masonry. Popular theory is that it was a smugglers' retreat, when Port Eynon was a thriving little port. But walling suggests much earlier origin. May have been stronghold-cum-columbarium for Port Eynon Castle, of which there is now no trace, but mentioned in lawsuit records in the thirteenth century (*cf* similar walling at Carreg Cennen Castle, near Llandeilo). In early sixteenth century, reputed that the notorious John Lucas of Salthouse repaired and rebuilt 'Kulverd Hall' and used it as a stronghold and armoury, making access to it under the point by an underground passage 'whereof no man knew ye mouth thereof'. **SS465845**

CULVER HOLE 2. Bone cave of same name in NW Gower, 30 m (100 ft) W of *Bluepool Corner*. The remains of over 30 individuals were discovered here suggesting that the cave was used as a burial place during the Bronze Age. Most of remains in NMW. **SS405930**

CWM IVY Point of access to *Whiteford Sands* and *Whiteford Burrows* ½ mile N of *Llanmadoc*. A small group of houses down short lane alongside Llanmadoc Church. Parking in field (honesty box at gate). From here, access to Cwm Ivy Woods, *The Groose* and *Whiteford Burrows*.

In Cwm Ivy Tor, left of path, is a small cavern facing E - no recorded archæological interest. **SS438937**

DEBORAH'S HOLE Small bone cave approx ½ mile W of *Paviland Caves*, high in cliffs above inlet formed by *Horse Cliff* and *the Knave*. Finds from cave in SM. **SS434863**

DEEPSLADE (NT) A rocky bay between Pwlldu Head and High Tor, distinctive for its geological formation. Excellent example of sequence of raised beaches and glacial deposits. *Bacon Hole* W of the bay has evidence of Iron Age and later Roman occupation. Also known as Hunts Bay as the farmland (Hunts Farm) sitting above was given by William de Breos (Norman Lord of Gower) to his huntsman William de Hunde. You will also find below a rocky step, difficult of access, a memorial to the poet Vernon Watkins who lived nearby. One mile E of Southgate bus terminus. **SS563868**

DELVID *Llangennith* farm overlooking *Broughton Bay* and Burrows. **SS424928**

DEVIL'S BRIDGE See *Worms Head*.

DEVIL'S KITCHEN Small bone cave W of *Foxhole*.

DILES LAKE 'Lake' is Gower word for stream. The small river flows past Coety Green, appearing eventually on Rhossili beach. According to Wynford Vaughan Thomas, it marks the coastal boundary between N and S Gower. **SS411912**

DRUIDS MOOR On the S-facing flanks of *Hardings Down*, below *Cathan*. **SS440900**

DUNVANT (Dwfn-nant – deep stream) Village and suburb of Swansea. Formerly a busy minor industrial centre with coalmines and brickworks, all now silent. Valley was cut by overflowing of meltwater at the close of the Ice Age.

Combined cycle- and FP uses route of former railway line through *Clyne Valley*. At the site of the former Dunvant railway station stands a memorial to miners killed at the nearby Killan Colliery in the disaster of November 1924 when five men died from flooding.

FPs to coast at *Blackpill,* to *Gowerton* and inland to *Three Crosses*. **SS595937**

DYKE (THE) See *Groose (The).*

EYNON'S FORD Old Gower settlement on N edge of Penrice Woods, near an old crossing of Penrice Stream. Said to be named after George ap Eynon of Brynfield, Reynoldston in seventeenth century, but name is recorded earlier.

One legend tells how a swarm of thousands of *verry* (fairy) folk came one night to the farm, slaughtered an ox in the very sight of the farmer, skinned it, then sat down to a feast and ate it all up except, of course, for the bones. They then proceeded to fit it together again, so that the whole ox was restored except for one tiny leg bone. They hunted for this in great agitation, but in vain. From that day on, the ox was no worse for it, except for a slight limp on that leg. **SS488887**

FAIRWOOD COMMON First open space on main road out from Swansea via Sketty and Killay. At *Upper Killay* (5 miles W of Swansea) built-up area suddenly gives way to open moorland and long views of Gower and *Cefn Bryn*. Road forks here to form two main routes into the peninsula, south road (A4118), to *Port Eynon*, *Rhossili* and bays on S coastline; north road (B4271), to *Llangennith* and N Gower villages. Both roads end in cul-de-sacs at the coast and there are few links between them. Tradition has it that the route of the south road was established by a farmer driving an ox plough across the common from a turn at Vennaway Lane, near *Kilvrough*, on the original road and then up to join the north road at *Upper Killay*.

Fairwood Lodge, once called Killay Lodge is a mainly Georgian house which has been the residence of the Principal of Swansea University and also the

Judges' Lodgings for the local Circuit.

For 2 miles Fairwood Common and Swansea Airport lie between the two roads. The runways cover two Bronze Age barrows or 'burches', cinerary urn now in SM. **SS568920**

FAIRYHILL Lies among the narrow sunken lanes alongside the Burry Pill, at the W end of *Cefn Bryn* and near to *Burry Green*.

One of Gower's few large country houses, much restored in recent years and now part of Gower's popular wedding industry. Once a fine residence, formerly owned by the Lucas and the Benson families. Lady Barham lived here in 1814 and was instrumental in establishing six Calvinistic Methodist chapels in Gower. **SS467912**

FALL BAY (NT) Secluded sandy bay near *Rhossili*, in shelter of limestone cliffs and *Tears Point*, and separated from *Mewslade Bay* by the NT headland of Jacky's Tor. Accessible, on foot only, from *Middleton* (1 mile), around headland from *Rhossili* (2 miles) or across sands at low water on spring tides from *Mewslade Bay* ½ mile E. Sands, cliff walks, fishing.

Fine exposure of Pleistocene raised beach. Good fossils in limestone on W side of bay. Iron Age promontory fort on Lewes Castle, magnificent cliff E of bay. **SS413874**

FELINDRE Interesting village in *Mawr* containing 1896 Nebo Chapel, with its murder stone and a corn mill of eighteenth-century origin. Blaenant-ddu dam (built 1860-1878) taken out of service in 1919. **SN640027**

FORESTER'S CAVE See *Foxhole*.

FOXHOLE Small rocky bay in Pennard cliffs. A fine example of a patella beach composed of layered sand, rounded limestone, fossil fragments held together by calcareous cement. Forester's Cave W of Foxhole. Large rhinoceros bone found here. Devil's Kitchen is a small bone cave W of *Foxhole*. Track to Minchin Hole, 365 m (400 yds) E, begins here. **SS553872**

FOXHOLE SLADE Located in the cliffs between *Port Eynon* and *Rhossili*. A stone-strewn valley leading down to *Paviland Caves*.
SS439858

FROG LANE See *Llanmadoc*.

FROG MOOR At foot of W slopes of *Cefn Bryn* (½ mile W of *Reynoldston*). Open land, marshy in places, with views of W Gower. Crossed by road, *Reynoldston* to *Fairyhill*, and various tracks.

FPs to *Knelston* (½ mile S), *Burry Green* (1 mile W).
SS470905

GANDER STREET Roadway from *Oxwich Green* to *Oxwich* passing near to *Oxwich Castle*.
SS496864

GIANT'S GRAVE (or Parc le Breos Tomb shown on map as Long Cairn).

Neolithic tomb in Green Cwm (½ mile N of Parkmill). Well preserved chambered long barrow (approx 3500 BC). Restored by the former Ministry of Works. Remains of about two dozen human beings found in 1869. Probably built originally on bank of stream, now flowing underground. For access, see *Cathole* 1. Remains in University Museum of Oxford.
SS537898

GOWER HERITAGE CENTRE is a visitor attraction based around a working twelfth-century water mill. There are craft shops, craft activities, an old fashioned games arcade, a sandpit area, adventure playground, a soft play area, a tractor play area and an animal area. Also home to La Charrette, Wales's smallest cinema. See *Parkmill*.

GOWER'S LOAD on Bryn Common, S of *Llanmorlais*. Coal was sent all over Gower from Llanmorlais and the name may derive from this business. The old coal way down to the mines on the Wern can still be followed as FP. **SS529936**

GOWERTON (Welsh – Tregŵyr). Also previously known as Gwter Felen or, when the railway came, as Gower Road. Up to the mid nineteenth century this was little more than a cluster of cottages, a water mill and some farms. It developed rapidly as an industrial centre with collieries and metal works. The Elba Colliery, begun in 1881, had a disastrous explosion of firedamp in 1905 and eleven men were killed. The colliery supplied the Elba Steelworks, which finally closed in 1967. Gowerton is now a busy village and shopping centre at E end of N coast road (B4295). Railway station. **SS590963**

GOWER WAY STONE Large boulder on E end of *Cefn Bryn* above *Penmaen*, placed to mark the route of the Gower Way (a Gower Society project for the Millennium) which crosses the Lordship of Gower from *Rhossili* to *Penlle'r Castell*. A plaque on the stone was unveiled by HRH The Prince of Wales in July 1998 to inaugurate the Gower Way. There are 50 stone markers on the 34 mile long path which takes in some of the finest and most interesting aspects of the Lordship of Gower. Keen walkers should also note that the Wales Coastal Path takes in the entire length of the Gower coastline. See also *Cefn Bryn*. **SS523888**

GRAVES END A circle of limestone, visible when undergrowth dies back, on E side of Pwlldu Head, marks mass grave of 68 bodies following ship wreck of the *Caesar* in 1760. The ship had a press gang crew from Swansea going to fight in the Seven Years' war with France. The point at which the ship struck is a recess between massive rocks known today as Caesar's Hole. See also *High Pennard*. **SS572864**

GREAT TOR Spectacular spur of cliff formed by vertical limestone strata, separating *Three Cliffs Bay* from the 2½ mile sweep of *Oxwich Bay*. Popular with experienced climbers. To the W, crowned with a stile on the footpath, are Honey Tor and also Little Tor.

Leather's Hole is a bone cave high up on Great Tor.

Difficult access from above, via gap between two humps on headland. Remains in SM. Benrick is the prominent tidal rock just off *Penmaen Burrows* E of Great Tor.

See also *Tor Bay.* **SS530877**

GREEN CWM See *Llethrid Cwm.*

GROOSE (THE) W end of Llanrhidian Marsh (NT) and much dissected by water channels. A sea wall was built over 200 years ago to reclaim the nearby Cwm Ivy Marsh. After the salt had leached away, the resulting fresh water marsh was fenced off into fields. The sea wall, known locally as The Dyke, was breached and the area flooded in 1974; the wall was heightened in an attempt to prevent a recurrence. Regrettably, the latest breach (in 2014) is denying access along the path to Whiteford Burrows, part of the Welsh Coastal Path. **SS446944**

GUZZLEHOLE (or Guthole) See *Bishopston Valley.* **SS575884**

HAEL LANE Welsh 'heol' means lane, like *Poundffald* an instance of English and Welsh names coexisting – joins Hael Farm with East Cliff and Southgate. **SS560877**

HANGMAN'S CROSS Where a number of ancient tracks meet on the roadway from *Penrice* to *Moor Corner* (at 1 mile W of Penrice). This roadway is believed to follow the route of an old road from *Rhossili* to *Oxwich*. Old Sheep Lane is now a bridleway to *Oxwich*. Probably a gibbet was once erected here, at least one body being buried in nearby Grave Lane. Moorhouse Lane is a bridleway to *Scurlage*, across what, until the 1680s, was a large common known as Porteinon Moor. See also *Merrysun, Bryn-sil, Beggars Pit*. **SS483867**

HARDINGS DOWN One of three Old Red Sandstone hills in this area of Gower. Remains of three Iron Age hill forts dating back 2000 years found here. House platforms with cobbled entrance and pottery found dating back to 150-100 BC. **SS437906**

HARESLADE Wooded slade or valley behind *Brandy Cove*. Lower Hareslade Farm on lane leading to main road at *Pyle Corner*. Upper Hareslade Farm is on high land above the valley. **SS584877**

HAYES WOOD (Hayes – Gower word for an enclosed field). On lower slopes of *Cefn Bryn*. Part of the woodland of *Penrice* to N of *Home Farm*. **SS496892**

HEATHERSLADE A small rocky bay ¼ mile W of *Foxhole Bay* Pennard. Nearby in 1960s a worn bronze bowl filled with 2583 Roman coins was discovered dating back to Valerian, known as the Pennard Hoard. Also location of a nursing home, on the site where the Gower poet Vernon Watkins lived as a young man with his parents. **SS549873**

HELWICK BANK also known as Helwick Sands, see *Port Eynon*.

HERONSTREET Roadway leading from *Oxwich Green* to *Eastern Slade* (½ mile W) where lane continues down towards *Slade* Bay and *The Sands* on the W side of *Oxwich Point*. **SS490860**

HIGH PENNARD 1. E limit of Pennard Cliffs. Evidence of Iron Age fort. Now dwellings look over *Pwlldu Head*. In 1760 survivors of the wreck of the *Caesar* made their way up to this lonely spot to raise the alarm. See *Gravesend*.

2. A promontory fort on cliff top, overlooking *Hunts Bay* (NT).

FPs down to *Bishopston Valley* and *Pwlldu*. **SS567866**

HIGHWAY On main road from *Pennard* Church to Southgate, location of two farms – Great Highway and Little Highway, once home of notorious smuggling family the Arthurs, and track leading down through *Bishopston Valley* to *Pwlldu Bay*, called Smugglers Lane. This sunken lane enabled contraband to be taken from Pwlldu Bay to Highway. **SS559884**

HILLEND House and farm with popular camping and surfing spot N end of Rhossili Down. Cannons in the garden said to date pre-1700, but too worn now to verify. **SS418910**

HOLT'S FIELD See *Manselfield.*

HOLY'S WASH Short stretch of coast between *Slade* and *Oxwich Point*. **SS495853**

HOME FARM Large main farm of the Penrice Castle estate, on south road (A4118), opposite W gates of Penrice Park. Current home of the annual Gower Show in early August. The buildings represent the best example in Gower of a model farm. Attractive raised granary across road nearby.

See also *Kittle Top*. **SS495890**

HONEY TOR See *Great Tor.*

HORSE CLIFF On coastal FP *Port Eynon-Rhossili*, to W of *Paviland Caves*. Seen from Rhossili side, rising above *the Knave*, this is one of the most striking cliffs in Gower, the dip of the limestone strata being almost vertical. This is the only point on the coast where no rocks are uncovered at low water. Iron Age promontory fort on W of cliff top.**SS435860**

HORTON Seaside village at E end of *Port Eynon Bay.* From the top of the village the lane descends 60 m (200 ft) to sea level in ¼ mile. Dunes, sands, rock pools, canoeing, fishing, walking. The Inshore Lifeboat Station was established in 1967. Methodist chapel. Est 1813. Holiday accommodation and caravan sites. CP, toilets, FPs from lower village to Port Eynon (½ mile W), Oxwich (4 miles E). Also old Gower tracks at top of village via *Hangman's Cross* to *Penrice* (2 miles W), *Reynoldston* (4 miles NW). **SS474857**

HUNTS BAY See *Deepslade.*

ILSTON (from Welsh – Llan Illtyd Gŵyr). Hamlet in wooded valley of Ilston stream. This is one of the most ancient sites in Gower and still one of the most tranquil. The former quarry nearby is a nature reserve. St Illtyd's Church is possibly the least known in the peninsula and gives the visitor an impression of incredible antiquity. Part of the church was restored in 1998. It would appear from a reference in the Book of Llandaff that a Christian cell was established here during the early sixth

century called Llancynwalan. Probably the early Llan was abandoned and later re-established by, or transferred to, the mother church at Llantwit Major and dedicated to St Illtyd. A late fifteenth-century rector, William Smith, became a Bishop. The present building grew out of an earlier chapel and probably took on its present form in the later middle ages. This parish was granted to the Knights Hospitaller, who retained it until 1540. Between 1540 and 1863 the Lord Chancellor had control, after which the parish passed into private hands. A medieval bowl can be seen in the porch and in the chapel an unusual triangular-topped wall recess. In the nave is the pre-Reformation bell, which was removed from the tower in 1974.

Hoard of 91 Roman coins found in quarry in 1933. Now in SM and NMW. FPs to *Parkmill* on south road (A4118). Narrow metalled lanes to *Lunnon* (1 mile W) and to north road (B4271) near *Cartersford Bridge* (1 mile N). **SS557905**

ILSTON CWM Delightful little valley of the Ilston stream, known as the Killy-Willy. The name, said to be of Irish origin, has also been given to an area of woodland and fields overlooking the site of the early pre-Reformation chapel (see below). The name possibly reflects the stream's rapid, twisting course down to *Parkmill*, reaching the sea eventually at *Three Cliffs Bay*. At Trinity Well, ½ mile from the Parkmill end, are foundations of the first Baptist

Church established in Wales (1649-1660) with a memorial to founder John Myles, once rector of *Ilston*. At the restoration of the monarchy in 1660 John Myles was ejected. Like the Pilgrim Fathers, after 1663 Myles took 18 of his congregation to the New World for religious freedom, founding the settlement of Swansea in Massachusetts.

Close by are traces of foundations of a pre-Reformation chapel. FP to *Ilston* (1½ miles N) begins at gate on main south road (A4118) alongside the former Parkmill School, now the West Glamorgan Guide Activity Centre. **SS553896**

ITALY See *Moor Corner.*

JACKY'S TOR (NT) See *Fall Bay.*

KEENMOOR LANE See *Pitton Cross.*

KENNEXSTONE At road junction between Llangennith and Llanmadoc. Site of farmhouse built in 1610, dismantled and rebuilt (1955) at St Fagans National Museum of History near Cardiff. Typically painted vivid red to protect against evil spirits. **SS450916**

KILLAY (Welsh – Cil-le, a narrow place) Extensive residential area, PHs, petrol, shops, St Hilary's Church, Siloam Baptist Church, bowls, tennis. Main road dips steeply to cross Clyne Valley at the former LMS railway line (and the Railway Inn), now a cycle/FP to *Blackpill* and *Dunvant*. *Clyne Valley* is a country park, with access from Killay, *Dunvant* and *Blackpill*. Considerable quantities of war materials were brought along the railway track and into Swansea Docks in preparation for the D-day landings during WWII. Near the former Killay brick works, a short distance south along the cycle/FP, are two well preserved pillboxes originally built to guard the railway line.

See *Upper Killay.* **SS602929**

KILLY-WILLY See *Ilston Cwm.*

KILVROUGH MANOR (Pron.- Cilfrew) ½ mile SW of *Fairwood Common* on main south road (A4118). Imposing mansion in six acres of private grounds. Built by Rowland Dawkins in 1585, this is possibly the original manor house of *Langrove*. It was rebuilt in the eighteenth century. Until the late nineteenth century, the estate was run as a hunting estate.

Early in the nineteenth century Mrs Green, the Asian widow of the owner Major Green, made it known that she intended to carry out the custom of her country and place herself, along with the body of her dead husband, on a funeral pyre and ordered a quantity of wood to be prepared for that purpose. However, after a great furore in the area, she eventually consented to a funeral at Pennard Church.

Later in the century, Thomas Penrice, the second owner of that name, set about developing the estate and built the high wall surrounding it, as a shelter for his kitchen gardens at the side of the road down to *Parkmill*. This same Thomas Penrice also built Parkmill School and various farms and encouraged the building of the Gower Inn on the site of the male workhouse. The corresponding female workhouse was at the other end of the village near to the present-day *Gower Heritage Centre*. Kilvrough was purchased by Oxfordshire County Council and for several decades since then it has been used, effectively, as one of their residential centres for outdoor education.

Langrove was formerly a substantial farm, part of the ancient manor already in existence in the days of Edward II (fourteenth century). Now a leisure facility on the south road (A4118) across *Fairwood Common* on the site of a nineteenth-century keeper's cottage.

Cannisland is a residential site of mobile homes nearby.

Vennaway Lane (part of the B4436 road). Name given to section of roadway linking A4118 road over *Fairwood Common* with the *Southgate* road near *Pennard* Church. This was part of a very early road from S Gower through *Bishopston* to *Blackpill*.

Near the A4118 junction is a well preserved example of one

of the many Gower limekilns **(SS564895)**, reminders of what was once a major local activity. Also, at the junction, the grove of trees contains a Gower Society commemorative plaque. A round tower in field W of Kilvrough Manor is a folly with no public access, built by a former owner. **SS559893**

KIMLEY MOOR Farm on B4247 road 1½ miles E of *Rhossili*. **SS439875**

KINGSHALL Farmhouse ruin at foot of E slopes of *Rhossili Down*. A green way (Kingshall Lane) leads towards *Llanddewi* (2 miles E). This may have been an ancient roadway opening on to the downs, with paths S to *Rhossili* and N to *Llangennith*. The open field between Kingshall and *Old Henllys* is called Furzy Whole Moor, recalling the name of a hamlet of four houses, Whole Moor, which once lay to the N of Kingshall Lane.

There is little to account for Kingshall's grand name, but it was once owned by a branch of the powerful Lucas family.

See *Old Henllys*. **SS435892**

KITCHEN CORNER Little, sheltered inlet under National Coastwatch Institution station at *Rhossili*, immediately to E of S tip of *Rhossili Bay*.

Quarrying in the last century has left its mark all along this headland. Limestone used to be shipped from these 'flotquars' to Somerset and Devon. The winch of a former quarry and an early twentieth-century boathouse are still in place. **SS402875**

KITHEN WELL (sometimes Kitchen Well) One of the ancient wells of Gower, it is actually a spring as are many of the Gower 'wells'. In the hollow alongside the road to the forestry car park at *Green Cwm*. **SS539886**

KITTLE On W side of *Bishopston Valley* (NT). Houses around what remains of a village green, a junction of roads leading to *Parkmill* and to *Fairwood Common*. Shops, PH. The old main road descends sharply and turns up again over a ford near *Bishopston* church; this road is now best covered on foot. The modern road to Parkmill (B4436) follows a less steep course but has a wide sweeping bend beside Barland Quarry. FP, S to *Bishopston Valley* and *Pwlldu*.

Kittle Hill Lane runs towards Fairwood Common and passes the large Stonegate Poultry Farm. See *Barland Common*. **SS574893**

KITTLE TOP (or Kettle Top). Huge rounded grassy mound alongside main south road (A4118), 180 m (200 yds) W of Penrice *Home Farm*, probably of glacial origin. The site is crossed by a FP between *Reynoldston* and *Mill Wood*. **SS493888**

KNAB, THE also known as Knab Rock. Slipway at *Southend*, *Oystermouth*. On coastal FP/ cycleway, also FP to *Mumbles Hill*. CP, PH, café, toilets. **SS626876**

KNAVE, THE Remarkable conical rock, dominating inlet W of *Horse Cliff* and ½ mile W of *Paviland Caves*. Smaller rocks on seaward side known as The Bull and Calf. **SS432862**

KNELSTON (Knoyle's Farm). Small settlement of some antiquity on a conspicuous rise on A4118, 1 mile SW of *Reynoldston*. Shop, petrol, small caravan site.

Ruins of church of St Taurin (twelfth century) in field behind present school. Later known as Llan y Tair Mair (Church of the Three Marys). It was already in ruins in seventeenth century. The name is supposed to come from the surname de Bien Savoir, some-time lords of the manor; this was translated into English as 'Know-well's ton', which became Knoylston or Knelston.

Three fine standing stones near here: one, the Knelston Stone, a little N of above ruin; the other two, Burry Eastern and Burry Western Stones, are one mile to NW. Trumpet Lane is an old Gower lane between Knelston and Burry Head. Central section is not open, but a public right of way on foot runs alongside lane.

FPs to *Burry* (2 miles N) and to *Berry* (1 mile S). See *Stouthall.*
SS467890

LAGADRANTA The location of the Llanmadoc Caravan and Camping Site, formerly a farm overlooking Broughton Bay. The name appears to be an Anglicisation of an obscure Welsh name. The origin may be Llygad rhandir, 'llygad' meaning the source of a stream and 'rhandir' referring to the landshares typical of medieval open-field system of farming in Gower. There is a legend telling how the farmer's wife lent a sieve to an old woman whom she believed to be of the 'verry' folk (Gower fairy). In gratitude the old woman offered an endless supply of beer, as long as no one knew of this. Unfortunately the farmer's wife could not keep the secret, and the beer ran dry!
SS428930

LANDIMORE N Gower hamlet descending steeply to the salt marshes 1 mile E of Cheriton. The ancient manor of Landimore was the administrative centre for much of W Gower in medieval times – *Bovehill Castle* being the last remnant of the manor house. The lower part of the village was called Underhill but the castle was Abovehill. In more recent times there were extensive limestone quarries along the edge of the Burry Estuary and the village operated as a small port, exporting lime and importing coal. Turn seawards off Oldwalls-Cheriton road.

See also *Groose, Loughor Estuary.*
SS465931

LANGLAND BAY (Long Land, a reference to the former strip fields). Popular beach, within a short distance of Swansea, patrolled in summer by lifeguards. Picturesque bay with immediate hinterland residential. The beach huts are a unique feature; these are day huts, leased for the season from the local council. Good sands, boating, walking, with excellent coastal views from cliffs in each direction. Popular with surfers and golfers. Tennis. Restaurant and cafés.

The romantic-looking mock-Gothic building overlooking the beach was built as a summer villa for Henry Crawshay, son of the Merthyr iron-master, Richard Crawshay. Formerly called Llan-y-llan (the name is apparently meaningless) and later known as Langland Castle, it was enlarged to become the Langland Castle Hotel and then the original Langland Bay Hotel. For a time a miners' rest home, now luxury apartments.

The Hole in the Wall shop in the middle of the bay once housed the water pump used in the supply of sea water to the hotel for salt water baths.

The E end of the bay is known as Rotherslade or, sometimes, as Little Langland, which can be reached on foot along the promenade from *Langland Bay* or by road from Langland Corner on the *Oystermouth* to *Caswell* road. A very deteriorated reinforced concrete structure which formerly housed a café, dance hall and sun deck has been replaced by a series of landscaped terraces and steps which lead down to the bay.

Fine cliff walks to *Mumbles Pier*, via *Limeslade* (1½ miles E) and to *Caswell* (1½ miles W).

Parking. Seasonal dog ban 1st May-30th September.
SS607874

LANGROVE Former site of fourteenth-century manor, now location of campsite and leisure facilities.

See *Kilvrough Manor.*

LEASON A small and ancient hamlet in N Gower, a mile to the W of Llanrhidian. Interesting ruins and spring below on the edge of the marshes. FPs to *Weobley Castle* (1½ miles W) and along edge of salt marshes to *Landimore* (1 mile E). **SS483925**

LEATHER'S HOLE See *Great Tor.*

LEWES CASTLE See *Fall Bay.*

LIMESLADE BAY Sheltered pebble beach, some sand when tide out; small inlet ½ mile W of Mumbles Head. There are many '..slades' – a Gower name given to a green, often gorse-covered, usually dry, limestone valley opening out to the sea.

Walled-in entrance to old iron ore working (worked

perhaps even by the Romans) can be seen at head of bay. Many housing developments, especially in Plunch Lane, which leads to Mare's Pool and Thistleboon.

CP above *Bracelet Bay.* Café and restaurant. Seasonal dog ban 1st May-30th September. Cliff walk to *Langland (*1½ miles W). Past *Tutt Head* to *Mumbles Pier* (½ mile E). Walks inland around *Mumbles Hill* with good views.

SS626870

LITTLE REYNOLDSTON
Small hamlet on left of minor road leading to *Reynoldston* village just off A4118.
The former farm of Little Reynoldston originally dates from the late 1500s or early 1600s. **SS489893**

LLANDDEWI (Church of St Dewi). Ancient settlement with church and manor house, ½ mile W of *Knelston*, 1½ miles SW of *Reynoldston*, a little along *Burry Lane*. Seen from rise of Knelston, the church and few farm buildings stand out strikingly against the hills of W Gower.

In medieval times a number of family seats were concentrated here: *Scurlage, Old Henllys, Brynfield,* also *Kingshall.* The Church of St Dewi is probably the least symmetrical in the peninsula but has dignity and charm. The origin of this church could be during the Celtic Church period and it appears to have been part of the estates belonging to the Bishop of St David's from its founding until 1923.

There have been two major restorations (1876 & 1905) which, although retaining a few earlier features, removed more notable ones such as a seventeenth-century squire's pew.

As far as the building itself is concerned, it has an unusual alignment in which the chancel deflects to the south – a weeping chancel. The reason for the misalignment can only be conjectured. Note the medieval scratch sundial.

Castle Farm, opposite church, sometimes thought to be the manor house, is a substantially modernised medieval house built by the Mansel family in the sixteenth century. Pevsner's 'Guide to Glamorgan' connects this with the site of the Bishop of St David's Palace.

See *Old Henllys, Scurlage, Kingshall, Burry.* **SS460891**

LLANDEILO TALYBONT (Welsh – Church of St Teilo at the end of the bridge) Original large and important Norman twelfth-century motte and bailey castle visible on the S side of the M4 motorway as it approaches Pontarddulais. The castle was built by Henry de Villers soon after 1106 and was probably attacked by the Welsh in 1116 and again destroyed in 1215, though rebuilt by 1319 when the 'tower of Talybont' is recorded. The castle and settlement were built on the River Loughor at an important crossing point from the W into the Lordship of Gower. The medieval church of St Teilo, of pre-Norman origin and N of M4, was dismantled in the 1980s and rebuilt (with colourful, replica wall paintings) at the St Fagans National Museum of History, near Cardiff. **SN585029**

LLANGENNITH (Welsh – Llangenydd) Not a coastal village, but located on third corner of NW Gower at the end point of the north road (sixteen miles to Swansea), PH (accommodation), caravan and camping sites with restaurant. Witness of many shipwrecks, which villagers were quick to exploit. Once a thriving village with cockfighting, weaving, gaming and much more. Villagers took a vote during WWI to decide if Llangennith should put the clocks forward an hour as did the rest of the country. They agreed to give it a month's trial. Now a popular destination for the excellent surfing at nearby Rhossili and Broughton Bays.

The village divides into West Town and Priorstown. The latter relates to St Cenydd's

Church, the largest in Gower. It is believed to have grown from the church of Llangennith Priory.

This church is specifically named in an early grant recorded in the Book of Llandaff and was reputedly founded by St Cenydd in the sixth century. It was a bangor (college) of sufficient importance for its destruction by the Vikings in the tenth century to be recorded in the Chronicle of the Princes. Shortly before the Norman invasion, a church was consecrated here and five monks ordained by Bishop Herwald. On the W wall of the church is a tenth-century ornamental slab which is said to have covered St Cenydd's tomb. A thirteenth-century effigy can be seen near the font, and the previous existence of a rood loft is indicated by an elevated opening in the chancel arch. This was the largest of the churches on the Gower Peninsula and formed part of a Benedictine Priory under the Monastery of St Taurin in Normandy. In 1414 it was seized as an alien Priory and was given to All Soul's College, Oxford in 1441, which owned it until 1838. Adjoining the church, on the lane to *Coety Green*, is College Farm, which is on the site of the original priory buildings. Opposite the lych gate on the green is the ancient village well, restored in 1998, with faint traces of an early cross cut into its stone cover.

FPs to *Rhossili Sands* (1 mile W), *Broughton Bay* (1 mile N), *Bluepool Bay* (1½ miles NW), and across hills to *Rhossili* (3 miles S), *Llanmadoc* (1½ miles NE). See also *Hillend*.

SS426915

LLANGIWG The ancient church of St Ciwg stands amid outstanding upland scenery above the Swansea Valley. The religious community responsible for the first building on this site probably existed in the earliest period of the Celtic church. The substantial stone building that we now see has its origins in the Norman period and some remains, as in parts of the tower, can still be seen. The picturesque lean of the tower was more alarming before it was reduced in height and, in 1812, the whole building was substantially refurbished and re-roofed. In 2007, the building came into the private ownership of the Friends of Llangiwg, a voluntary organisation comprising members of the local community.

Inside the church is the head of a tenth-century wheel cross; this has been tentatively associated with the Gellionnen stone in SM. **SN723056**

LLANGYFELACH This church stands on the site of an early monastic community. Bishop Cyfelach died *c* 750 AD fighting the Saxons. Bishop Herwald consecrated a church here during the second half of the eleventh century but how long this building lasted is unknown. The medieval building was severely damaged by a gale in 1805 and the church, apart from the tower, was demolished about 1830. The old tithe barn, now the nave, was converted into a church. Within the church is a lettered and decorated cross slab together with a seventeenth-century memorial brass erected by the Puritan Marmaduke Matthews. A ninth/ tenth-century cross base, originally close to the old tower, has been moved into the nave of the church – the stone carving is notable. A wall tablet in the N chapel records the change from the Julian to the new Gregorian calendar in 1752. In the churchyard is a tenth-century cross base close to the tower.

PH on the village green.
SS646990

LLANMADOC (Church of St Madoc). N Gower village overlooking the *Burry Estuary*, on the slope of *Llanmadoc Hill*. Not a coastal village but access to sea and sands to W and salt marshes to N. The village is mostly strung out along Rattle Street which is said to be named from the sound of weaving looms in cottages along the lane. The street descends past *Frog Lane* towards *Cheriton*. Frog Lane, which is now a track leading towards *The Groose,* was once a hamlet off main road as it descends in the direction of *Cheriton*.

For many years a Christian Youth Holiday Camp has existed here. Once a lively weaving centre; some of the reconstructed woollen factory in St Fagans National Museum of History came from here. A house called The Factory is a reminder of the trade.

The Church of St Madoc is reputed to have been founded in the sixth century. From the presence of an early inscribed stone it can be presumed that the date of the original Llan is prior to 550 AD. The present building dates from the thirteenth century but underwent extensive restoration in 1865. Set in the cill of the nave window is a lettered stone, which intriguingly displays Gallic as well as Irish characteristics in its formulation and dates from the period 450 – 550 AD. In addition to this stone commemorating 'Advectus son of Guanus', there are in the W wall a crude pillar cross and a boundary marker, both of which come from the period 600-900 AD. The present font is probably late Norman. A rood loft entrance can be seen in the chancel arch.

This church was given to the Knights Templar in 1156, but on their suppression it passed, like many other of their churches, to the Knights Hospitaller in Herefordshire, who retained it from 1309 until their dissolution in 1540. From 1540 until 1920 the incumbents were appointed by the Prince of Wales. The bell dates from 1675.

PH, community shop with PO and café, caravan site.

See also *Cwm Ivy, Spritsail Tor, Lagadranta.* **SS440934**

LLANMADOC HILL At 186 m (610 ft) one of the highest points in Gower, formed of Old Red Sandstone: a landmark in W Gower, also known as *Llanmadoc Down.* Some fine views from the top and from the approaches down to village. At E end earthworks known as *The Bulwark*, also some Bronze Age cairns. Fragments of cinerary urn in SM. On the lower slopes, at the

Cheriton end of the hill, are the remains of the old Llanmadoc schoolhouse.

FPs, and lanes to *Broughton Bay* (1 mile W), *Whiteford Burrows* (½ mile NW) and across hill to *Llangennith* (1½ miles SW).
SS430925

LLANMORLAIS (Welsh – Glanmorlais, on the banks of the Morlais stream). A village of nineteenth-century miners' cottages, farms, Tirzah Baptist chapel (recently fallen out of use) and more modern housing. Once the terminus of the railway from *Gowerton,* it was a centre of considerable mining activity. Even in Tudor times this was a busy mining area with coal passing through the village in panniers on donkeys, bound for vessels in the estuary beyond. It is now connected with the cockle industry at nearby *Crofty*. **SS529947**

LLANRHIDIAN North Gower estuarine village sloping steeply down to the salt marshes. Approach road at junction of the north road from *Cillibion* (B4271) and road from *Penclawdd* (four miles to NE) – B4295. Once a centre of weaving (see *Staffal Haegr*) and sheep rearing. Large flocks of sheep used to be kept on the marshes and today salt marsh lamb is much valued for its flavour. There are new buildings but the character of the old village remains.

The ancient Church of St Rhidian and St Illtyd is situated beneath a limestone bluff, and its massive W tower is dwarfed only by the neighbouring cliff. The date of the original Llan may well be prior to 550 AD, as at one time there was reputedly an inscribed stone of early sixth-century type in the vicinity. 'Rhidian' may be a corruption of Tryrulhid, the name of St Illtyd's wife. The present building dates from the thirteenth century, but underwent extensive rebuilding in 1858. This church, together with a chapel at *Walterston*, were granted to the Knights Hospitaller in 1167, who retained them until 1540. From then on the incumbents were appointed by Lay Patrons until 1923.

On the tower roof is a large stone block, which is thought to have been used as a hearth for beacon fires. A grotesquely carved stone believed to date from the ninth century may be seen in the porch. Known as The Leper Stone, it is a massive block of stone, bearing simple representations of human figures and animals carved on one face. It was dug up in the churchyard in the nineteenth century and was moved to the protection of the porch about 1910.

A standing stone (conglomerate) mounted on a limestone base on the green may be the remains of the village cross, and is said to have been used as a sort of pillory before the nineteenth century; it was re-erected in 1821 by the villagers, who erected its limestone partner in 1844.

Butter Well is an ancient well in a private garden near Llanrhidian Church. From 1185 there are legends that a copious stream of milk and butterfat issued from it. Known also as St Illtyd's Well.

There were two mills on the tiny stream which runs through Llanrhidian; now only Nether Mill remains. The iron wheel had gone by the 1960s, but the mill building, on three floors, with an attractive mill pond alongside, are of interest. A tablet below the large stone chimney indicates that the year of building was 1803. Petrol, PH, restaurant. FP below cliffs to *Weobley Castle* (1½ miles W). The lane E along the salt marshes was once the main road to Llanmorlais. See *Cilifor Top.*

SS497923

LLETHRID Small sheltered farming settlement on north road, B4271, at W limit of *Pengwern Common*, 4½ miles W of *Upper Killay*. Here the road twists and descends steeply into a little wooded valley to cross the upper stream of the Parkmill Pill, before the stream enters *Green Cwm* and disappears for part of its way underground.

Near the old lodge house of the former *Parc le Breos* estate, beside the bridge, is the entrance (now sealed) to Llethrid Swallet, on private land. This is a large limestone cave with a wealth of stalagmites and stalactites, some of rare mud formations. The fragile calcite deposits and mud formations are amongst the few recorded in Britain.

FPs S to *Green Cwm* and *Parkmill* near bridge, and WNW to *Cillibion*. **SS530913**

LLETHRID CWM or Parc le Breos Valley or Green Cwm is a delightful wooded valley, 2 miles long, stretching from *Parkmill* N to *Llethrid*. A public FP runs through the valley, passing near *Cathole Cave*, the *Giant's Grave* and a restored limekiln near an old quarry. The valley is formed in limestone; its stream now runs underground from Llethrid, and is thought to reappear at the water pumping station at the Parkmill end of the valley near the CP.
SS530913 – SS538896

LLIW VALLEY RESERVOIRS (Cronfeydd Lliw). An 1860 Act of Parliament authorised the building of the reservoirs to supply Swansea with water. Work began on the Lower Lliw Reservoir in 1862, under the scheme of eminent Victorian engineer, Robert Rawlinson. It was completed in 1867 and the smaller Upper Lliw Reservoir followed in 1895. The Lower Lliw Reservoir, extending over 13 ha, has a capacity of 269 million gallons.

The Gower Way links the two reservoirs with scenic and interesting walking through a variety of habitats. CP and an excellent café/shop (open all year except Christmas) at Lower Lliw Reservoir. Signposted on the B4489 (Felindre) from M4 junction 46. **SN649035**

LLWYN Y BWCH Old farm to S of *Oldwalls*, now a wedding venue. Once associated with the Gordon family, an ancient family of *Weobley Castle* and NW Gower. **SS484916**

LONG CAIRN See *Giant's Grave*.

LONGHOLE CAVE Bone cave high on Overton Cliff,

1 mile W of *Port Eynon Point*. Reached by a rough track from above or below. Take FP above rocks from *Overton Mere* or follow Overton Lane to end, then stone wall for 365 m (400 yds), descend slade towards the cave about 40 m (45 yds) above HWM.

Considerable animal remains and implements in SM and British Museum. **SS451850**

LOUGHOR Very important historic borough, the site of two consecutive Roman forts of the first and second centuries AD. Later, a Norman castle (early twelfth century), the motte and later stone tower of which are freely accessible. Both military installations commanded the lowest crossing of the River Loughor, the castle controlling access into the Lordship of Gower from the W. From the road bridge there is a pleasant public walk N along the tidal reaches of the estuary. Upper Loughor, Glebe Road – Moriah Calvinistic Methodist Chapel, associated with Evan Roberts (1878-1951), important Welsh preacher and revivalist. PH and shops.

SS564980

LOUGHOR, RIVER AND ESTUARY (also known below the road bridge as the Burry Estuary to Inlet). Gower is bounded on its N side by the estuary of the Loughor River, a river which drains approx 250 sq miles of the surrounding area. The flats and marshes are formed by the River Loughor after it has been joined by the Dulais, the Llan and the Lliw, that descend from the hills to the N. They are rich in flora and wild life and offer a complete contrast to the cliffs and bays of the peninsula's S coast. This is a major location for wading birds and the marshes are utilized mainly for grazing by semi-wild ponies where formerly there were cattle. Sheep still graze.

The sands are also important to the local cockle industry, centred around *Crofty*, although this has declined in recent years. There have been cockle pickers here since the earliest times. Up to the late twentieth century, the business of gathering and preparing cockles was a cottage industry. The cockles live in the soft and muddy sand of the estuary and were raked out and sieved to remove undersized cockles. After washing, the cockles were put into sacks, which were carried back to the villages on the backs of donkeys or by pony-drawn carts. They were then prepared for market in small back-garden boiling facilities. In more recent times the donkeys have been replaced by tractors or landrovers and strict legislation with regard to health and quality means that the boiling of the cockles is carried out in processing plants at the marsh edge. Currently the industry is going through a very hard time, because, for reasons unknown, local cockles are not reaching maturity. Cockles brought long distances by road from other fisheries keep Gower's factories in production.

LUCAS BAY See *Oxwich Point*.

LUNNON (Welsh – Llwyn-onn, ash grove). Hamlet above *Parkmill*, linked by lane with *Ilston* (½ mile NE). Approach road, continuing to *Pengwern Common*, leaves A4118 road at *Parkmill* and ascends hill sharply. **SS548898**

MANSELFIELD Formerly a separate hamlet which until 1880 formed a detached part of the parish of Nicholaston; now an eastern continuation of *Murton* towards *Newton*.

Nearby Holt's Field is a community which has developed from one of the many chalet sites built in the area between the two World Wars. **SS594888**

MANSELFOLD Farm in N Gower. The close association of the Mansel family with Gower is recalled by several place names.

The Mansel family, one of the ancient families of Britain, arrived with William the Conqueror (name derives from Le Mans). It has had connections with Gower ever since. For complete pedigree of family see J D Davies's 'History of West Gower'. Among famous members of the family was Sir John Mansel, who was Lord Chancellor to Henry III (thirteenth century). **SS475919**

MANSEL JACK See *Samson's Jack*.

MARGAM FARM At the W end of the lane known as Margam Lane, which leaves main Port Eynon road at *Moorcorner*, at junction with road to *Horton*. The often muddy track, which has a turning to *Overton* half way along it, emerges onto the main *Rhossili* road (B4247) at Margam Corner, ½ mile E of *Pylewell*. For walkers only, it is a short cut between the villages. This is part of an old drovers' road into Swansea, via *Penrice*. The name recalls direct connection between the Mansels of Penrice and Margam Castle, near Port Talbot, which eventually became their home. **SS452868**

MAWR Upland area of the Lordship of Gower, extending N from the M4 motorway. Initially as enclosed pasture becoming open moorland, including 'free to roam' mountains of Mynydd y Gwair, Mynydd Pysgodlyn and Cefn Drum. Mawr comprises much of interest including the *Lliw reservoirs*, the settlements of *Felindre* and Graig Cefn Parc and the bridge at picturesque Pont Llechart with nearby Cae Castell (a medieval ringwork castle, possibly the only example of Welsh castle construction in Gower – **SN688045**). The area is crossed by the *Gower Way* and other scenic walks such as along the fast flowing Lower Clydach River.

See *Penlle'r Castell, Lliw Valley reservoir.*

MAYALS Now a suburb of Swansea at the E edge of *Clyne Common*. Formerly known as Le Mayals. Mayals Road runs alongside the municipal park of Clyne Gardens with its extensive collection of rhododendrons and large bog garden.

See also *Blackpill* and *Clyne Valley.* **SS608903**

MERRYSUN Name of former farmhouse, now renovated, near *Horton*. Also, a section of *Penrice* parish. Possibly named after an ancient inn which stood near here. Also known as Cold Comfort. **SS477872**

MEWSLADE BAY (possibly from mew: seagull) (NT & SSSI). One of the smaller bays near *Rhossili* immediately W of *Thurba Head* and possibly the most spectacular bay in Gower, with outstanding rock scenery.

Good sands, completely covered for two or three hours around high water. Reached by a moderate walk through a typical Gower slade. Worth noting are extensive stretches of very recently restored limestone walling throughout this area, some of which restoration/ maintenance is supported by the Gower Society.

In a small quarry on W side of valley, bones of six or seven humans found in nineteenth century. On opposite side, nearer the sea and 40 m up (130 ft) is the small Mewslade Cave where signs of human habitation have been found. Artefacts in SM. The valley is partly owned by the NT. Access is by FP from CP (privately owned) and bus stop at *Pitton*.

SS420872

MIDDLETON Important part of *Rhossili* parish (½ mile E of church), with village hall. There used to be three inns in Middleton, but now there are none. The last, the Ship Inn, is now Ship Farm, next to the village hall. The area has connections with Edgar Evans who was born in Fernhill Top, a cottage in School Lane, where there is a blue plaque commemorating him. He died on Scott's last expedition to the South Pole in 1912. There is a memorial to him in Rhossili church. Bus stop, limited parking by hall.

FPs to *Fall Bay*, to *Mewslade*, and path across *Rhossili Down* to *Llangennith* (3 miles N).

SS422878

MILL WOOD An article in *Gower Journal* in 1959 contained the statement '. . . Mill Wood is gone. Where it stood there is a bald and scarred hillside in the heart of Gower . . .' Fortunately the woodland has re-grown in the intervening years and we can again enjoy the many pleasant walks to places such as *Bryn-sil Top* and the vanished hamlet of Capon's Hill. The old mill pond and mill leat can be examined as well as the ruin of the mill building and the ponds, which were part of an early fish farming operation. The mill ruin stands at the bottom of Penny Hitch, where tradition has it that horses, with hire charge of one penny, used to be kept to help carts up steep hill.

SS490883

MINCHIN HOLE The largest of the coastal caves and SSSI, situated in the cliff face 550 m (600 yds) SSE of the *Southgate* bus terminus, below a small but prominent limestone knoll. The cave has been extensively excavated in recent years, and has produced remains of elephant, bison, soft-nosed rhinoceros and hyena, as well as traces of human occupation in more recent times.

Accessible with care and some scrambling. Remains in SM.
SS555867

MONKSLAND Farm near *Scurlage*. The name reflects the close proximity of *Paviland,* which was a grange of the Cistercian Neath Abbey.
SS459877

MOOR CORNER At junction of main *Port Eynon* road with road to *Horton* and *Penrice*. This is E end of Margam Lane and beginning of FP to *Rhossili*. The name recalls the long vanished Porteinon Moor, which stretched for almost a mile N and E of this spot. The open moorland was enclosed piecemeal by neighbouring farmers between 1680 and 1690. The main road between Moor Corner and Scurlage was sometimes known as Italy.
SS464865

See also *Margam Farm.*

MOORMILLS A large sink hole on *Cefn Bryn* W of *Broad Pool*. Formed by the collapse of land into a cavern in the underlying limestone. In the nineteenth century it was frequently recorded as flooding and overflowing onto the common. Although several streams empty into it, Moormills is a dry sinkhole.
SS506913

See also *Broad Pool.*

MOUNT HERMON See *Penclawdd.*

MOUNTYBANK See *Penrice.*

MUMBLES (possibly from Fr mamelles: breasts). Prominent twin limestone islets marking W extremity of Swansea Bay. Both accessible at low water, but watch the tide! On the outer islet are the lighthouse, built in 1793, and a coast defence fort of 1861. Mumbles Pier is nearby, at the end of which a new lifeboat house was opened in 2014. The old lifeboat house was built in 1920. Usually the name is given to the whole of this end of Swansea Bay, including *Oystermouth* and Southend. At the Pier a CP now occupies the site of the terminus of the former Mumbles Railway, the first in the world to carry passengers, and which was closed in 1960. The railway ran to Swansea along the coast as far as *Blackpill* and then on the landward side of the golf course and alongside the Mumbles Road as far as the vicinity of the present St David's Car Park. A promenade now follows the track bed as far as Blackpill sharing the space with a cycleway from Southend onwards. After Blackpill the combined pathway continues along the track bed of the former LMS line into Swansea, so providing a continuous route around the bay.

In the 1870s, the outer island was the scene of very early experiments in overwater telegraphy conducted by J D Llewelyn of Penllergare and Professor Sir Charles Wheatstone, which anticipated by many years Marconi's experiments with radio further up the Bristol Channel.

CPs, cafés, amusements, PHs, accommodation, shops, toilets, public transport links. Yachting and rowing clubs. Two lifeboats.

SS635871

See also *Oystermouth*.

MUMBLES HILL High ground behind Bracelet Bay, site of many anti-aircraft installations during WWII and now a nature reserve with views over Swansea Bay and the Bristol Channel.

See also *Knab Rock*. **SS627873**

MURTON Now part of *Bishopston* with a village green and well. Farm with shop and plant nursery and some old cottages remain with many new developments. The Methodist chapel, opened 1879, was extended in 1998. The village has both community and chapel hall. Once a centre for market gardening and laverbread manufacture. PO/shop, PH. Approach road at W end of *Clyne Common* off B4436, otherwise through Bishopston (½ mile W) along narrow lane. **SS588890**

MYNYDD BACH Y COCS (Welsh – cocos, cockles). Stretch of common land, source of Morlais river SW of *Three Crosses*. The remains of Whitewalls Colliery, which operated until 1948, can be seen at the E end of the common. The ruin of Carmel Chapel (1889) lies beside the road near the W end. Many FPs radiate from the common towards *Three Crosses*, *Blue Anchor* and *Gelli Hir*. **SS558935**

NEWTON 1. Formerly a separate village community, now virtually joined to *Oystermouth*. Enlarged by recent development, but with much of its basic street plan and character remaining. The village once stood in the centre of an area of long, narrow fields derived from the enclosed strips of a medieval open field settlement. The chancel of St Peter's church contains a memorial tablet to hymn writer Frances Ridley Havergal (see *Caswell*), who helped teach at nearby Paraclete, the fourth of Lady Barham's Gower chapels, erected in 1818. Installing her secretary, William Hammerton, as minister caused a rift with the Calvinistic Methodists. It is now a Congregational Chapel. During her stay in the village, Frances Ridley Havergal played the organ and taught in the Sunday School – a framed photograph of her hangs inside the chapel, and the lectern is in her memory. At the top of Caswell hill a plaque is outside the house, now re-named Havergal, where she died in 1879. **SS603882**

NEWTON 2. Farm ruin near *Pilton Green*. As early as 1840 Newton Farm was being worked with Pilton Green and is now split between *Margam Farm* and Great Pitton Farm near *Rhossili*. **SS452880**

NICHOLASTON Coastal strip between *Cefn Bryn* and the sea, reaching to about 1 mile W of *Penmaen*, each side of the A4118 road. The houses, scattered farms and a few guest houses enjoy a variety of landscape probably unrivalled in Gower: on the seaward side, Nicholaston Woods, *Three Cliffs Bay* plus much of *Oxwich Bay*, and behind, the slopes of *Cefn Bryn*.

E end of Nicholaston Woods is locally known as Crawley Woods, a few minutes' walk from Nicholaston Cross (½ mile W of Penmaen) down towards sea and *Oxwich Bay*. Unusual combination of beach, cliff, dune and woodland. There is an Iron Age promontory fort on the small headland overlooking burrows and the sharp finger of rock known as Crawley Point, near the FP, high up at edge of Crawley Woods, marks an excellent view point above *Oxwich Bay*.

The church of St Nicholas stands isolated from rest of its parish on a busy winding stretch of the south road (A4118). Remains of an alleged earlier church lie covered by the sand dunes below the village. The present church's predecessor on the same site is thought to be of fourteenth-century date and within the porch is a medieval tombstone. The church was restored by Miss Olive Talbot of Penrice in High Church tradition in 1894, in memory of her father C R M Talbot of Margam Castle. Materials used for the interior included teak and oak, alabaster and coloured marble. The font is said to be made from a solid block of stalagmite, and the hanging pulpit (as opposed to one attached to the floor) is decorated with alabaster figures of John Keble, Edward Pusey and Henry Liddon, Anglo-Catholic clergy prominent in the Oxford Movement. The antiquarian Rev J D Davies, rector of

Llanmadoc and Cheriton, described Nicholaston Church as 'the most elaborately treated ecclesiastical building in Wales, if not in the west of England'.

At one time *Manselfield* was attached to this parish and it is one of the few Gower churches where lay patronage existed in medieval times. Camping, caravan park, farm shop. **SS523884**

NORTH HILL TOR (known locally as Nottle Tor). Prominent limestone headland overlooking marshes of the *Burry Estuary* ½ mile N of *Cheriton*. The site is occupied by massive defensive earthworks which, from its scale, suggests a pre-Roman Iron Age hill fort rather than a twelfth-century Norman castle. The site is in private ownership. **SS453937**

NORTHWAY Part of *Bishopston* at W limit of *Clyne Common* and near junction of the road to *Murton*. Petrol station and shop. **SS585894**

NORTON 1. Former hamlet off Mumbles Road NW of *Oystermouth*, now swallowed up in urban development. The neo-classical Norton House (1790) is, at present, a restaurant and hotel. **SS614886**

NORTON 2. Farm and former medieval settlement high over Oxwich Bay on lane linking Oxwich Castle with Penrice. Within the grounds of Norton Farm lies the original timber ringwork castle at Oxwich, an early twelfth-century foundation. The castle, built on two levels, is the largest surviving example of a ringwork castle in Gower. Site in private ownership. **SS492867**

NOTT HILL (NT) Small but prominent hill overlooking *Three Cliffs Bay* on W side. Superb views over this bay. Accessible by lane (the former parish road) from green on top of Penmaen Hill. **SS535885**

NOTTLE TOR See *North Hill Tor.*

OLD HENLLYS (Welsh – Hen llys, old court). Locally known as Hentlis. A remote farmhouse 1 mile W of *Llandewi*, along the wide, green *Kingshall* Lane. Once a manor house, seat of the Mansel family. Much of the old walling can still be seen. Outside chimney typical of old Gower houses. Behind house, capacious cellars, said to have been built by the Mansels for concealing contraband goods. An underground passage is said to have linked these cellars with *Rhossili* (over 2 miles away!).

In fields beside the lane from Old Henllys to *Llandewi* the ruins of small limekilns and quarries can be seen. Many farms produced their own lime to reduce soil acidity. Marl was also dug here. Marl is a clay material rich in lime which was also used as a soil improver.

FPs to *Hardings Down* (1 mile NW); to *Pilton Green*. Lane continues W to the ruin of *Kingshall* farm (1 mile W) and *Rhossili Down*. **SS449890**

OLD SHEEP LANE See *Hangman's Cross.*

OLDWALLS Hamlet 1 mile W of *Llanrhidian*. Two standing stones in fields nearby. Ebenezer Presbyterian Chapel was originally a Wesleyan building. FPs *Leason* (½ mile), *Llanrhidian* (½ mile N), *Cefn Bryn* (½ mile S). **SS488919**

OVERTON (a settlement on a bank – from OE *ofer* and *tun*). Secluded hamlet of *Port Eynon*. Lane turns off main road near top of Port Eynon Hill (½ mile from village). No through road for cars, but FP continues to join Wales Coastal Path onto cliffs for *Paviland* and *Rhossili*. Nearest access to sea (on foot) is at far end of hamlet, by lane to *Overton Mere*. **SS462853**

OVERTON MERE (NT) Sheltered pebbly beach W of Port Eynon Point, reached by track around Port Eynon Point, FP from *Port Eynon* or by lane from *Overton*. See *Culver Hole*. **SS464848**

OXWICH (variously attributed to Norse *ax*, water; *wick*, creek or *wich*, salt or *wic*, farm). Small seaside village of some antiquity, along lanes at W end of a magnificent 2½ mile sweep of sands. Guest houses, shop (seasonal), refreshments, hotel, restaurants, caravan parks. Once small port exporting limestone. Two castles nearby. A community largely by-passed by the heavy holiday traffic to the bay. There are many picturesque cottages in traditional Gower style. In the eighteenth century John Wesley stayed in one of these cottages during his visits to the area. The Wesley cottage can be seen on the right about 90 m (100 yds) from junction with the marsh road.

One of the charms of the Church of St Illtyd lies in its site, half hidden by trees on the hillside by the sea. This church stands on ground reputedly sacred since the sixth century. The present building is probably of thirteenth-century origin but underwent restoration *c* 1890. A noted seventeenth-century rector of this parish was Hugh Gore who founded the Swansea Grammar School in 1682. This is one of the few Gower Churches where medieval incumbents were appointed by lay patrons. For a reason not readily apparent, *Nicholaston* and *Manselfield* were part of Oxwich Parish. The church contains monuments from the thirteenth and fourteenth centuries, one of which, the De La Mare effigy, is made from sand and plaster. When a portion was analysed, it was revealed that it was made from local sand which had been cemented together with plaster and then covered with a painted plaster coat. Within the church is an ancient font and a fourteenth-century bell, together with two gravestones of the same period. **SS499865**

OXWICH BAY A large, privately-owned CP and beach, (public access), dominates the approach. Its accessibility makes it, with *Port Eynon*, one of the most popular beaches for boating. There is a vast curving expanse of sand, with a rich and colourful background of sand dunes, salt marshes, woodland, with cliffs at each end and *Cefn Bryn* in the background. These provide a variety of plant and bird life rarely found in Britain. Use special care towards all wild life here; this is a National Nature Reserve. Nature trail leaflets are available. The visitor needs to be aware that, in recent years, the S edge of the bay has been subject to significant rock and land falls which affect access.

The large old building on the foreshore was used in the past to store coal delivered into the bay by sea. Now a restaurant. Slight traces of the Coal Road can still be seen together with the route taken by bathing machines from Penrice House.

FPs around Oxwich Point to *Horton* (4 miles W), *Port Eynon* (4½ miles W) via *Slade* (3 miles W).

Lanes through village to *Penrice* (1½ miles), thence to Horton (3½ miles). Another through *Oxwich Green* to Slade (1 mile). Walks across sands or dunes to *Crawley Woods* and *Tor Bay*.

The best approach to Oxwich is a steep narrow road from *The Towers* on main A4118 road; the beginning was an ancient sunken lane on E side of Penrice Park, which then crossed marshes and meres (1½ miles in all). During WWII the road, known locally as The American Road, was improved to allow access to the beach for military vehicles. This resulted in a large area of the dunes being flattened.

The original salt marshes were drained in the nineteenth century to provide farmland in a much praised enterprise. However, lack of manpower during wartime resulted in the neglect of the drainage system which can still be seen today.

OXWICH CASTLE The castle is not readily seen as it stands high above the village amongst the trees, but there are fine views from it over the bay towards *Pwlldu Head*. It is an important sixteenth-century fortified manor house, open to the public (Cadw). Its late date, vast areas of living accommodation and relatively weak defences show that the building could more accurately be described as a mansion than a castle. Its buildings stand around a roughly square courtyard, entered through a simple but impressive gateway, which bears an heraldic plaque with the arms and initials of Sir Rice Mansel (1487-1559). The castle gateway was the scene of a violent incident in 1557, when during a dispute over goods recovered from a wreck, followers of Sir Rice Mansel clashed with those of Sir George Herbert, steward of the lord of Gower. Anne Mansel, sister-in-law of Sir Rice, was mortally wounded by a stone thrown by one of Sir George's followers. This serious matter reached the Court of Star Chamber, and the legal records cast a detailed if lurid light on this dispute between two leading gentry families.

Pigeon House, Oxwich Castle

The remarkable medieval Oxwich Brooch, found here in 1968, is on display in the NMW. To the NE of the Tudor manor house lies an old tower, which is probably medieval and the forerunner of the present Oxwich Castle. The tower is on private land. **SS4978863**

OXWICH GREEN Little, wind-swept settlement, ½ mile S of the main village. The road continues through Oxwich Green to *Slade*. A few guest houses and CPs.

FPs to Oxwich, *Horton* and *Hangman's Cross*. **SS495860**

OXWICH POINT The second highest headland in Gower at 85 m (250 ft). Protects *Oxwich Bay* from the SW winds, but the remains of some of the many wrecks may still be seen on its weather side.

Lucas Bay, a small shingle bay between *Holy's Wash* and Oxwich Point. **SS513850**

OYSTERMOUTH (See also *Mumbles*) Name said to derive from Welsh: Ystumllwynarth and was recorded as Ostreme in 1284. *Oystermouth Castle* dominates the skyline here. Older parts of village straggle up the steep limestone cliffs and were built when quarrying, iron ore working and oyster fishing were thriving occupations here.

The Church of All Saints is built, possibly, on the site of a Roman villa. The three bells that once hung in the church tower bear inscriptions in Spanish dating from the eighteenth and early nineteenth centuries. They were brought from the gutted cathedral of Santiago de Cuba by one of the Swansea copper ore barques and were presented to the church *c* 1865 by Mr Aubrey Vivian. In 2010 they were returned to Chile. There has been a church at Oystermouth since Celtic times as this church is mentioned by Nennius (ninth-century Welsh monk). It is probable that there was a Llan here before the ninth century. The N aisle of the present building was the original church until it was enlarged in 1860. Following the Norman occupation of Gower, the church was granted to the Abbey of St Peter at Gloucester. In 1367 the church was transferred to the Hospital of St David in Swansea, which retained it until 1540. Rev Thomas Bowdler, whose expurgated editions of Shakespeare gave rise to the expression 'bowdlerising', was buried here in 1825.

Within the church can be seen, amongst other objects, some fragments of Roman mosaic, an early font and a pillar piscina. Stained glass in the church reflects the strong links with the lifeboat community.

Entertainments are held in holiday season within the castle grounds. Watersports centre at nearby *Knab Rock*, Southend. Hotels, restaurants, shops, cafés, many PHs and guest houses. PO, shops, CPs on seafront and in quarry. Public transport links to Swansea.

SS616882

OYSTERMOUTH CASTLE

This magnificent castle dominates the landscape. It is likely that a timber castle was established here soon after 1100 probably by the de Londres family, who also held Ogmore Castle. The castle and manor of Oystermouth came into the direct ownership of the lords of Gower, who used it as an alternative to Swansea Castle as a residence, fortress and prison. It was then progressively restructured in stone. As with other castles in Gower, Oystermouth suffered in various Welsh attacks during the twelfth and thirteenth centuries, but was repaired and extended. Much of what remains today was the work of the de Breos family, and was probably completed in time for the visit of Edward I in 1284, on his triumphal tour of Wales following the defeat of Llewellyn 'the last'. Within three years of his visit, the castle was taken during a forlorn but fierce Welsh rising. The castle was repaired and extended again (*c* 1310) by the building of the massive NE tower. The top floor of this contained a fine private chapel, with traceried windows, which are still prominent features. This tower is now a visitor facility. The castle remained in the hands of the chief lords of Gower, serving as a country seat, courthouse and prison for several centuries, but in 1650 it was described as *'an old decayed castle . . . being for the present of noe use, but of a very pleasant scituaton and near unto the sea side'*. Recently refurbished by Cadw. **SS6156882**

PARC LE BREOS A secluded country house, 1 mile W of *Parkmill*. It stands surrounded by Park Woods and takes its name from the private hunting ground of the Norman family of de Breos, which held the Lordship of Gower in the thirteenth and fourteenth centuries. The course of this old park boundary bank can be traced for nearly 6 miles. Later, in the nineteenth century, the park became part of the hunting grounds for the Vivians. Currently a restaurant with rooms.

A grove of trees in Park Woods was planted for the Golden Jubilee of the Gower Society in 1998. See *Green Cwm*.
SS529895

PARKMILL Here the A4118 runs in a steep-sided narrow wooded valley and the village of Parkmill lines the road from the mock-Gothic former school house to the Park Mill itself, ½ mile W. The school is now the West Glamorgan Guides' Activity Centre. The mill itself, first mentioned by name in 1287, is now the centrepiece of the *Gower Heritage Centre*. Mount Pisgah chapel, established by Lady Barham (see *Fairyhill*), is also now a Visitor Information Point. Shop, PH, CPs (one is seasonal).

Stonemill is the E end of *Parkmill,* near Guides' Activity Centre, the former school, and the Gower Inn. See also *Kilvrough Manor.* FPs and bridleways to *Penmaen*, *Ilston*, *Three Cliffs Bay*. **SS550892**

PAVILAND Also known as *Paviland Manor* which was a

grange of the Cistercian abbey at Neath. Isolated farm, 2 miles E of *Rhossili*, lying between A4118 and sea. Entrance gate a few yards E of *Pylewell*. FP to cliffs and *Paviland Caves* along W edge of farmland, not by gate, but by stile marked by fingerpost on main road 130 m (150 yds) W towards Rhossili at *Pilton Green*. **SS446865**

PAVILAND CAVES Two caves in remote cliff face 2 miles W of *Port Eynon* and S of *Paviland Farm*.

Goat's Hole: one of the most famous bone-caves in Britain. Featureless at present owing to thorough excavations and not impressive in size, but with a fascinating pre-history and, archæologically, has been called 'the richest of British caves'. In 1823 a headless human skeleton was found by Dean Buckland, who named it The Red Lady of Paviland, because the bones were stained red and surrounded by ornamental bone rods. In 1913 an excavation by Prof Sollas established that it was of Palæolithic date. The skeleton is in fact male and is now dated by radiocarbon to *c* 33,000 BC. The red staining might result from burial rites, as a symbol of immortality. Remains of over 800 implements also found, together with bones of animals well suited to Ice Age climate. Interesting remains and a replica in SM but the original Red Lady is in Oxford University Museum of Natural History. The cave is difficult to find and access, unless correct path and tide conditions are chosen. FP from main road (finger post at edge of *Pilton Green*) ends at entrance to narrow craggy valley divided by stone wall. This can also be reached from *Wales Coastal Path* from *Port Eynon* (2 miles) or *Mewslade* (1½ miles).

Follow FP down E side of valley to rocky inlet. Cave is on opposite side of gully, facing sea, but because of difficulty in crossing gully, access is really only practicable on about 8 days in the month, *ie* two days each side of spring (very low) tides. The cave is visible from the flat rocks, about 9 m (30 ft) above sea level. The right hand (W) side of the valley is steep and dangerous; several people have been killed here.

Paviland W Cave: 45 m (50 yds) W of Goat's Hole and about same level above sea. Of no great interest. Fauna found possibly of Pleistocene origin.

Yellow Top is the limestone mass in which *Paviland Cave* is situated. An Iron Age promontory fort stands on top of this headland, defended on three sides by near vertical 45 m (150 ft) cliffs. On the landward side four lines of banks and ditches protected the small settlement which existed here 2,000 years ago. So called because of the yellow orange lichens on the rock face, which are more conspicuous here than on most parts of the coast.

SS437858

PENCLAWDD (Welsh – end/head of the ditch/earthwork). A large village of NE (Welsh) Gower. The name probably refers to the ancient hillfort of *Pen-y-gaer* on the hill above the village. Penclawdd began to develop in the seventeenth century and, by 1800, it was a thriving seaport with many coal mines and a copper works. The works of the Cheadle Copper Company manufactured, among other things, the bronze manillas which were currency for the slave trade. It revived briefly after a slump in the late 1800s, but most activity had stopped by 1900. The first of the Vivian family of industrialists, John Vivian, came from Cornwall and operated the works here in 1800 before moving on to land leased from the Duke of Beaufort at Hafod in the Lower Swansea Valley. There he founded a much larger enterprise. A railway served Penclawdd industry from 1866 to 1957, with a passenger service between 1867 and 1931. A canal was also built from *Waunarlwydd* to Penclawdd, opening in 1811, to bring coal from the hinterland. It was a failure, but remains of the canal dock still project into the marshes at the E end of the village. The village has a church, St Gwynour at Llan-yr-newydd, rebuilt in 1851. It was formerly a chapel-of-ease to *Llanrhidian* church and was probably medieval in origin. There are also three large chapels: Tabernacle Presbyterian (1836), Trinity Baptist, and Bethel Welsh Independent (1816). Bethel is a large chapel on the hillside; it was rebuilt in 1910 with an imposing neo-classical façade, but has been sold pending development. The congregation have refurbished the adjacent former Sunday School, with financial help from the Gower Society, winning a Gower Society design award for making a welcoming meeting place suited to their needs. Although several members are Welsh speakers, services are in English. The abandoned Mount Hermon Chapel standing on a hillside W of the village overlooking the estuary, was an early Baptist chapel (1807). In its early days it was painted white as a landmark for vessels navigating to Penclawdd and *Loughor*.

The cockle industry, for which Penclawdd was famed, is now centred on *Crofty* and *Llanmorlais*. The cockle women of the village were a notable feature of markets in Swansea and across S Wales; the money they earned provided an important contribution to the families of miners and metal workers in the village.

See also *Crofty*.

PENGWERN COMMON (SSSI) Undulating open land, flanking the B4271 road 3 miles E of *Llanrhidian*. With *Fairwood* and *Welsh Moor*, it lies on the boundary between English and Welsh Gower. **SS540920**

PENLLE'R CASTELL Important ruins of the early thirteenth-century stone castle built to defend Gower from Welsh attacks from the N. It is sited on the N border of the Lordship and at 373 m is the highest point in Gower with extensive panoramic views (albeit now somewhat interrupted by wind farm construction). The castle comprised two defended baileys each with a square stone tower. The castle was probably the site of the 'new castle of Gower' destroyed by Rhys Fychan, Lord of Dinefwr and Is Cennen in 1252. **SN665096**

PENLLERGAER VALLEY WOOD Now the site of the award winning Penllergare *(sic)* Valley Woods Project. Originally created by John Dillwyn Llewelyn (1810-82), a pioneer of photography, with its scenic woodland walks, lakes, astronomical observatory and much more, it is currently being restored by the Penllergare Trust. Site, nature trails and coffee shop are open to the public. CP. **SS630985**

PENMAEN (Welsh – stone head, end or top). Scattered village along A4118 1 mile W of *Parkmill*. Dominated by the former workhouse (built in 1861 and much extended). It is currently Three Cliffs Care Home formerly Glan y Môr.

The Church of St John the Baptist has an obscure history, but it seems certain that it stood on its present site in the fourteenth century. An earlier church in the burrows occupied a site overlooking *Three Cliffs Bay*. From the early thirteenth century, the church was under the Knights Hospitaller until about 1540. In 1854/5 the building was almost completely reconstructed, which left little of the original structure. It was during this restoration that an unusual genealogical seventeenth-century tombstone was discovered. The lineage on it extends back to pre-Norman times. This memorial is now set on a wall. When this site was excavated during the nineteenth century, the evidence found suggested that it had been abandoned in the early fourteenth century; some of the objects discovered during this excavation are preserved in SM.

Lane (from main road) to *Tor Bay* and Penmaen Burrows. Talbot's Road (see Cefn Bryn) can be followed from behind the Three Cliffs Care Home building. The Gower Way can also be followed onto *Cefn Bryn* passing the *Gower Way Stone*.
SS530888

PENMAEN BURROWS An area of blown sand, coarse grass and bracken above the 60 m (200 ft) limestone cliffs W of *Three Cliffs Bay*. The prominent tidal rock close to the shore is known as *Benrick*. Four sites of archæological interest are to be found on the burrows in close proximity to one another. They are:

Penmaen Old Castle On the cliff edge overlooking Three Cliffs Bay – a Norman timber ringwork castle of the twelfth century. It consists of a massive stone bank fronted by a deep ditch. Excavation here in the 1960s revealed remains of

stone and timber buildings, and recovered the plan of the timber entrance tower, which had been burnt down in a fierce fire. From here the ruins of Pennard Castle are visible across the bay to the NE.
SS535880

Penmaen Neolithic Tomb (also referred to as *Pen-y-Crug*) 230 m (250 yds) ENE of above site. A good example of a large communal tomb of the first farming communities to arrive in Gower. Probably 5,500 years old. Note remains of entrance passage, and one remaining side chamber. **SS532881**

Old Church This is near the track leading to Old Castle, and is within 140 m (150 yds) of the point where the lane from the main road opens on to the dunes. The first Penmaen church stood here, and now consists only of a stone-walled depression in the dunes. The nave and chancel can still be made out. It has been said that a whole village lies buried beneath the sand here. Other remains of the medieval settlement are visible from time to time as sand cover is blown away. **SS533882**

Pillow Mound This large artificial rabbit warren is a fairly recent discovery and is not recorded on older OS maps. Warrens such as this have been constructed since Norman times when rabbits were first introduced as a source of meat and fur. This particular warren might have been associated with Penmaen Old Castle or could have been constructed for the lord of the manor in medieval times. **SS534879**

PENNARD Now a densely populated village of Gower, it originally referred to the area near the only church, where there were few inhabitants. Pennard includes the residential area also referred to as *Southgate*.

The current church of St Mary replaced the original medieval church near the castle, 1½ miles to the W, which, with its surrounding deserted medieval village, was overwhelmed by sand incursions in the fourteenth and fifteenth centuries. Fragments of the earlier church can still be seen within the later building including the holy water stoup, now the font. There are also a Jacobean pulpit and font cover. The W tower is battlemented with corbelled bell housing. The church also contains a memorial to poet Vernon Watkins (1906-67) who used to live in The Garth on Pennard's West Cliff. The 50th anniversary of his death was marked by installing a memorial stone and planting a silver birch tree in the grounds of Pennard School, which, along with Pennard library, was opened in 1967. A smaller memorial stone to Vernon Watkins overlooks Hunts Bay, sited just below the clifftop, and a plaque outside what is now Heatherslade Residential Home states that he lived there before his marriage. Pennard churchyard also contains the graves of poets Nigel Jenkins and Harri Webb.

At one time the Manor of Paviland was part of this parish.
SS566886

PENNARD CASTLE
Originally an early twelfth century Norman timber ringwork fortification commanding the valley of the Pennard Pill, which leads down to the picturesque Three Cliffs Bay. The castle has a late thirteenth-century gatehouse, built into the defences of the original ringwork. The site of Penmaen Castle, across the bay, is visible from Pennard Castle. Castle is accessible to the public via FPs from the village.
SS544885

PENNARD PILL See *Three Cliffs Bay.*

PENNY HITCH See *Mill Wood.*

PENRICE The old village of Penrice (also Mountyborough or Mountybank) has twelfth-century origins and is dominated by a large Norman timber twelfth-century ringwork castle behind the houses to the W of the green. It was built by the de Penres family, who took their name from the area. The village, including the castle, Church of St Andrew, village green and surrounding burgage plots, is probably the best visible example of the new Anglo-Norman settlements in Gower. The castle is inaccessible and in private ownership.

The scene has scarcely changed since the eighteenth century. Once the social centre of Gower on market and fair days, with prize-fighting, stepping and rowdy high jinks. The charter to hold a fair is still valid. Accessible only by steep and narrow roads, with few passing places. Nearby is the pound, and the former village well is at the edge of *Mill Wood*. A large overgrown earthwork, the *Mountybank,* marks the site of the first Norman fortress of Penrice.

The Church of St Andrew has retained much of its ancient character. In the churchyard, near to the porch, is a gravestone for Mary Kavanagh murdered by an unknown hand in 1829 – the so-called Murder Stone. The building is of cruciform plan and probably of thirteenth-century date, but may incorporate earlier work. The church was under the Knights Hospitaller from the mid-twelfth century until their suppression about 1540. Later, lay patrons had control. Within the parish was medieval sanctuary land.

The building is noted for its very large porch, the inner door of which is hung on a free-standing structure. It is possible that this porch acted as a schoolroom during the seventeenth and eighteenth centuries. In 1893/4 the building was restored, but changes were not permitted.

The base of the village cross is still on the green but the cross itself disappeared during the eighteenth century. See also *Margam Farm*. **SS493879**

PENRICE CASTLE The stone-built Penrice Castle, lying within Penrice Park, replaced the nearby earlier timber ringwork castle at Old Penrice (Mountyborough) in the early thirteenth century. Its construction and enhancement at that time, comprising an imposing round keep and twin-towered gatehouse, makes it one of the most important and largest medieval castles in the region. The castle is in private ownership but is visible from nearby public FPs.

Below stands the modern 'castle', the only large country house of any age in Gower still used as a private residence. Built in the eighteenth century for Thomas Mansel Talbot, it is now occupied by the Methuen-Campbell family. The building is on four floors and has typical Georgian features, most notable being the massive, apse-like, stone bay window on the S side. A large Victorian wing was added on the E side of the main block but has been demolished. A waymarked public FP runs past the house between *Millwood* and the A4118. Close to this path, near the house, stands a small grove of trees planted over the years by royal visitors to *Penrice*. **SS497884**

PEN-Y-CRUG An earthen Bronze Age barrow north of *Cefn Bryn* and near *Broad Pool*. **SS511913**

PERRISWOOD Farm and hamlet N of A4118, ½ mile N of *The Towers* (a folly marking the entrance to *Penrice Castle*). Some of the houses were originally built for Penrice Estate workers. ½ mile E of the hamlet is Perriswood Archery and Falconry Centre (café, caravan site). FP to *Cefn Bryn* and *Penmaen*. **SS503887**

PILTON GREEN Scattered settlement 2 miles E of *Rhossili* where A4118 road opens out onto a small common (NT). Farms of East Pilton and West Pilton lie nearer Rhossili, between main road and cliffs.

FP to *Paviland Caves*, and to *Old Henllys* passing ruin of *Newton* Farm. **SS445872**

PITT Large, impressive farmhouse on lane between *Penrice* and *Oxwich*. Built in early seventeenth century, with drip-stones over windows and corbelled chimney. Once home of the Bennetts, a Gower family of some substance. References to Pitt as a landholding go back at least to 1516. **SS493871**

PITTON (Possibly – farm in a hollow). Sheltered settlement 1 mile E of *Rhossili*, centred around Great Pitton Farm, one of the oldest of Gower's farms. It has associations both with smuggling and with John Wesley. The Old Chapel Lane from B4247 road at foot of Pitton Hill leads down to *Mewslade* and Great Pitton, another in opposite direction leads up a little, wooded valley to Higher Pitton and FP across *Rhossili Down* to *Llangennith* (3 miles N). **SS428877**

PITTON CROSS Two farms on small common (NT) at top of Pitton Hill 1 mile E of *Pitton*. One farm is now a camp and caravan site. No crossroads, so possibly site of an ancient cross.

Keenmoor Lane is an old trackway leading from Pitton Cross to the back of *Rhossili Down*. FP and bridleway, via Keenmoor Lane, to Rhossili Down. **SS433878**

POBBLES BAY Popular small sandy cove accessed from Southgate or golf club, E of the well-known Three Cliffs Bay. Pobbles is safer to swim in than its neighbouring bay. **SS540877**

PORT EYNON (Welsh – Port Einon) The name is thought to be derived from Einon, who was one of the Welsh princes in the eleventh century. Early records suggest that there may have been a castle here.

The present village surrounds the church, with the houses on the side of narrow lanes extending to the beach. The church is dedicated to St Cattwg. Although the present building dates from the twelfth century, its origins are reputed to be in the sixth. From the twelfth to sixteenth centuries this church was under the control of the Knights Hospitaller. The earlier building was extensively renovated and enlarged in 1861, with a further restoration in 1901, but some of the ancient fitments still remain. Unusually, this church does not have an E window.

In the churchyard is a statue in Italian marble, commemorating the bravery and devotion to duty of three members of the crew of the local lifeboat *Janet* who died when the boat capsized while attempting to aid the steamship *Dunvegan* in 1916. This caused the lifeboat to be withdrawn, as it was considered too hazardous an area for its operation. The old lifeboat house at Salthouse Quay is now a Youth Hostel. An inshore lifeboat station was established at *Horton* in the same bay in 1968.

The area around Salthouse and the Port Eynon Youth Hostel is *Crowders Quay*. There is no direct road from the village itself to *Horton*, although it is linked by a bridleway. Likewise, *Overton* is either reached by FP or a turning off A4118, on right just before Port Eynon. Paint material obtained from a nearby mine was, according to the Penrice Estate accounts of the 1870s, the origin of the GWR livery of chocolate brown and dull ochre!

CP, shops, cafés, PH, Youth Hostel, guesthouses, caravan and camping sites. RNLI lifeguards operate on the beach in summer. There is a seasonal dog ban on the beach. FPs along coast to Horton (½ mile) and inland to Overton (½ mile).

SS468853

PORT EYNON BAY A fine curving mile of beach, with exposed prehistoric peat beds at the W end, fringed with dunes known as Burrows.

Like all impressive sands on this coast, it lies in the lee of a prominent headland, here Port Eynon Point. In the shelter of this point the past seafaring life of the village evolved; in front of *Crowders Quay* cottages, traces of the oyster pools and old quays can still be seen. At one time 40 oyster skiffs fished from here. In the nineteenth century limestone was quarried nearby and shipped across the Bristol Channel. The blue-green stones on the shore are not local; they were brought over as ballast by limestone ships from Devon. Smuggling, too, was a profitable occupation up to the end of the eighteenth century; allegedly there were at one time eight excise men stationed at Port Eynon.

PORT EYNON POINT (NT) is a good place from which to get a panoramic view of the whole of the bay, with *Horton* to the E, stretching on to *Oxwich* Point. To the W are the cliffs towards *Rhossili* and to the S, on a fine day, the cliffs of N Devon. The standing stone at the top of the headland is a memorial to Dr Gwent Jones and Stephen Lee, founder members of the Gower Society.

Off Port Eynon Point, to the W, lie the Helwick Sands or Helwick Bank, a dangerous sandbank which is 7 miles long and which has been the site of many shipwrecks. The name is derived from the Norse, meaning a covered or hidden town, and horseshoes have been dredged up here by the oyster fishermen in the past. Local tradition tells of a castle where a buoy now marks the E limit of the Helwick Sands. A lightship, which formerly marked the W end, is now part of the SM collections and is on display in Swansea Marina outside the NWM. It has been replaced by a radio buoy. Proposals in 1996 to double the amount of sand taken off the bank by commercial dredging have been the subject of much discussion, as the way by which sand moves between Gower beaches and Helwick Sands is not yet fully understood. It is feared that increased dredging results in a reduction of sand on these beaches.

Port Eynon Point Cave is at the tip of the point: a bone-cave about 6 m (20 ft) above sea level and inaccessible at HW. Track along shore W around *Salthouse Mere* leads to cave. Animal remains in SM and NHM.

See also *Salthouse, Culver Hole, Longhole,* and *Sedgers Bank.*
SS468844

POUNDFFALD (*Ffald* is Welsh for pound, so on translation: Poundpound, a mixture of languages due to its being on the border of old Welsh- and English-speaking Gower.) Poundffald is the W part of *Three Crosses.* A PH bears the same name as this part of the village; the remains of an ancient manorial pound for Subboscus (the Welsh-speaking NE of peninsular Gower) are incorporated into the building. In addition, it was the site of a tollgate on the old turnpike road up from *Penclawdd*; the area was one scene of the notorious Rebecca riots in 1843.
SS566945

PRIOR'S TOWN See *Llangennith.*

PRISSEN'S TOR (also known as Spritsail Tor). Distinctive limestone headland at E end of *Broughton Bay*. In the N face of the tor are two small caves linked by a low passage. These were discovered by two quarrymen in 1839. Animal remains, found in the caves in 1849, suggest that many thousands of years ago they served as hyenas' dens.
SS425937

PWLLDU (Welsh – black pool) Where *Bishopston Valley* meets the sea. A vast storm beach of limestone pebbles dams the *Bishopston* stream. Sands at low water. No access by car. The parallel bands and ditches which run down the steep slopes of the headland on the W of the bay and the pebbles of the storm beach are the relics of extensive limestone quarrying in the nineteenth century. This was once a community working the quarry. The two former PHs are now private residences; and the ruins of many cottages can be found in the surrounding woodland. Smuggled goods landed here were transferred to *Highway* farms in *Pennard*.

The Needles. Pwlldu

Access on foot from *Pyle Corner* (1 mile E), *Hunts Bay* (1 mile

W) and *Bishopston Valley*. FP up steps to *High Pennard*.
SS575871

PWLLDU HEAD Twin headland at SW end of Pwlldu Bay. Magnificent views E to the Glamorgan coast and W to Oxwich Point and further. Remains of an Iron Age fort on the W side, and on the E, Bantam Bay and the Ring Rock where 68 lives were lost on the shipwreck of the *Caesar* (see *Gravesend*). Limestone and smuggling were popular here. The late Nigel Jenkins, a much-loved poet of Gower, wrote a poem based on the shipwreck: *The Ballad of Pwlldu Head*.
SS560862

PYLE CORNER Between *Bishopston* and *Murton* where roads and FPs lead off seawards to *Brandy Cove* and *Pwlldu*. These roads are very narrow and not recommended for cars because there is no parking or turning space at the end. There is a shop near the main road.

See also *Bishopston Valley*, *Hareslade*. **SS580883**

PYLEWELL Group of houses on a rise in main road around old well 2 miles E of *Rhossili*. This is the E end of *Pilton Green*. Immanuel, one of Lady Barham's chapels (see *Burry Green*), which she had built in 1821, is now a private house.
SS448870

RAMSGROVE See *Thurba Head*.

RATTLE STREET See *Llanmadoc*.

RAVENSCLIFF Situated near *Southgate*, this is a cave where remains of mammoth, hippopotamus and lion have been found.

RED CHAMBER Sea cavern ½ mile E of *Thurba Head*. Of no interest archæologically; walls of cave colourful with red ochre, once extracted for commercial uses. At rear of cave, narrow tunnel made in search for lead in nineteenth century. Shaft at end, now filled with water. Can be reached from cliff path from *Mewslade*. Not accessible at HW.
SS426866

REYNOLDSTON The name of the village is said to derive from Reginald de Breos, an early Lord of Gower who died *c* 1221. Its growth was due to reliable springs and wells providing good drinking water. Almost at the centre of the peninsula, it straggles along the W slopes of *Cefn Bryn*, a pleasing village of greens and livestock, bracken, stone walls, little streams from the hill, and fine long views. This is a major meeting place of highways and byways from all over Gower.

Brynfield (or Brynefield) on the edge of the village, is one of the old houses of Gower. There seems to have been a substantial house here during the late medieval period. In Tudor times it was part of the Lucas family estate at Stouthall; during the mid-Victorian period it was the home of Sir Gardner Wilkinson, a distinguished Egyptologist and his wife, Caroline, who was a Lucas.

The King Arthur Hotel

The original PH overlooking the Higher Green, (the village having two greens), was the Rising Sun; the remains of this building may be seen near the present King Arthur Hotel.

St George's church has beauty and dignity. It is unusual for churches before the fourteenth century to be dedicated to St George and maybe the church had its original dedication altered. It was in private patronage prior to the Reformation. The present building was extensively restored during the second half of the nineteenth century and little of its earlier work remains, apart from a blocked lancet window in the chancel. This church now houses the circa ninth century pillar cross, which previously stood in a field beside the main road near Stouthall. The font is square and seems to have been made from a stalagmite. It is probably late Norman. One of the two bells in the gable is dated 1783; the other is unmarked. A Methodist Society was established in 1797, with the chapel built 70 years later. A stable was later added to the rectangular building for the visiting preacher's horse. That addition has since been converted into a kitchen, with a fine entrance porch added in 2003. The building is well used throughout the week, and the interior displays several colourful banners of Biblical verses.

Community shop with PO, PH. See *Arthur's Stone, Cefn Bryn, Stouthall, Eynonsford, Fairyhill.*

SS480900

RHOSSILI The origin of the name is open to much conjecture but the initial 'Rhos' seems to relate to a Welsh word for moorland.

Rhossili is usually bracketed with *Middleton*, *Pitton* and *Pilton*; the area forms a unique corner of Gower. In a relatively small place there is much to attract those interested in history, prehistory, flowers, rocks, seashore life, farming. Trees are very sparse and develop a wind-pruned shape. The landscape here is an almost treeless plateau and we are made conscious of the bare bones of the peninsula.

Even as late as 1900, Rhossili had changed little from previous centuries, when the main road ended at Pitton Cross. These days, the B4247 ends in the village, as does the bus service from Swansea. The houses are scattered around St Mary's Church, perched on top of the 70 m cliffs, at the most W part of Gower. *The Vile* is the medieval strip field system of Rhossili, extending from the church to the headland. It is a system of sharing out the best land in the parish. A large proportion of the land has been bought by the NT to safeguard the system. The relatively frost-free conditions suit the growing of early crops. The dramatic cliffs, headland and foreshore, including *Worms Head*, belong to the NT; the area draws over half a million visitors every year. The National Coastwatch Institution occupies the old Coastguard Lookout overlooking the crossing to Worms Head. It was initiated in 2007, the year after a man drowned when attempting to swim ashore from the Worm. The Lookout restoration was funded by the Gower Society.

On The Warren at the foot of Rhossili Down is the besanded church of Rhossili, which came under the control of the Knights Hospitaller during the twelfth century. The present church of Rhossili seems to be thirteenth-century, but it has the only carved late twelfth-century Norman doorway in Gower. Above the doorway, however, is decoration typical of the early thirteenth century. On the doorway stonework is a medieval scratch sundial and in the chancel a small fourteenth-century leper window can be seen. Within the church is a memorial to the local man, Petty Officer Edgar Evans, who died on the expedition to the South Pole (1912) led by Captain Scott. Just before Rhossili, in the hamlet of Middleton, a blue plaque hangs outside his birthplace at Fernhill Top, while SM contains a bust of him presented to the City of Swansea in 1994.

Walks radiate out of Rhossili in most directions: it is on the Wales Coastal Path, and the Gower Way starts at the Coastguard Lookout and runs through the village. The FP to *Fall Bay* starts opposite the church and passes through the Vile. There are paths down to the splendid beach and also up Rhossili Down (passing the old Rocket House, where up until early twentieth century, rocket equipment for bosun's chair rescues was kept). The most popular walk is SW down the track past the former Coastguard cottages, through the gate and alongside the drystone wall, passing the Old Castle Iron Age fort, and ending with the view over Worms Head. As on all Gower cliff walks particular care is needed if walking near the cliff edge.

There is a NT Visitor Centre and shop in the former coastguard cottages. The village has cafés, shops, toilets, CP, hotel with bar, holiday accommodation and a cliff rescue Coastguard station.

SS415880

RHOSSILI BAY The unspoiled beach is world-renowned. The bay is framed by the tidal islands of *Worms Head* at the S tip and *Burry Holms* on the N end; both islands are well worth a visit when the tidal conditions allow. It must be noted that the crossing to Worms Head can mean walking on rocky and slippery surfaces. Fatalities have occurred here and advice from the Coastwatch should be obtained before attempting a crossing at any time. The complete arc of the bay is 5 miles, the beach itself being 3 miles long. When the wind is high, the unbroken sand is often scoured by Atlantic rollers; so whether on a good day or a bad one, the view is spectacular and it is a popular surfing beach.

Tales of smuggling and shipwrecks form a link with the past; the wooden ribs of the *Helvetia*, driven ashore in 1887, can still be seen at the *Rhossili* end of the Bay. At the opposite end, during low water, part of the iron hulk of the *City of Bristol*, a small paddle-steamer homeward bound from Waterford which ran ashore in 1840, is visible. In the second half of the seventeenth century the 'dollar ship', reputed to have been carrying the dowry of a Portuguese princess (possibly Catherine of Braganza, who became the Queen of Charles II), was wrecked. In 1807 and 1833 quantities of silver coins were uncovered by the tides and found by villagers. Some of the coins, identified as Peruvian dollars of Phillip IV, still exist in SM and NMW.

At the raised terrace alongside the S end of the Bay is an area of sand dunes called The Warren, owned by the NT; during excavations in 1979 archaeologists discovered the remains of a lost village. Parts of a church and some houses were discovered; it is claimed that these could date back to pre-Norman times. The settlement is considered to have been abandoned in the early fourteenth century, most likely due to economic decline and gradual encroachment of the sand.

The isolated house near the centre of the raised terrace above the bay was an old parsonage, Rhossili Rectory; it was built when the living at Rhossili was combined with that at *Llangennith*. The present house, rebuilt in the 1850s, stands on a site which is thought to have associations with the Knights of St John. The Old Rectory was renovated in 1996, and is now a NT holiday house.

RHOSSILI DOWN At 193 m (632 ft), *The Beacon* (trig point) is the highest point in peninsular Gower; the climb is rewarded by 360 degree views of the peninsula, the Bristol Channel and Carmarthen Bay. Paths to the top start at *Rhossili* and there is also an easier climb from *Middleton*. As at *Cefn Bryn*, scattered stones, cairns and round barrows indicate the use of these hill tops as burial grounds over thousands of years. The oldest of all are *Sweyne's Howes*. A much more recent ruin, the former WWII prototype radar station, is situated in a hollow on the W slopes of the Down.

See *Burry Holms, Fall Bay, Kitchen Corner, Mewslade Bay, Paviland Caves, Pitton, Thurba.* **SS420895**

ROTHERSLADE See *Langland Bay.*

RYER'S DOWN Sandstone hill 114 m high between *Burry Green* and *Cheriton*. Some NT land. Extensive views across the Stembridge valley and N Gower. **SS458921**

SALTHOUSE Nationally important and rare survival of an ancient salthouse dating from the sixteenth century. The ruins are reached by FP, and lie at the W end of *Port Eynon Bay.* The industrial complex was sited here to take advantage of trapped sea water, which, with evaporation, has a high salt content. The ruins comprise salt-collecting reservoirs and a boiling house and pumping chamber. The site was later modified. The sea washes to the edge of the ruins, and at low water the remains of more massive structures, including heavy stone vaulting, can be seen on the nearby beach. These are all that the sea has left of a stone quay and salt pans which may have been part of the notable mansion of Salthouse, once a principal seat of the Lucas family.

The mansion remained in the hands of seven generations of the Lucas family, until it was severely damaged in a violent storm, probably the notorious Great Storm of 1703. The Lucases had become rich by a variety of means: sale of salt was one, another was the exploitation of paint material found on the land, others were reputed to be rather less legal! Two simple cottages were built on the site and they, in their turn, have fallen into ruin.

The award-winning site was

excavated by the Glamorgan-Gwent Archæological Trust and laid out for display in the late 1980s. Conservation work has been carried out on the ruins and the salt pans; information boards are in place. The works appear to have been demolished and the chambers filled in around 1650. **SS469847**

SALTHOUSE MERE is a small inlet under *Port Eynon Point* separated from the bay by a ridge of rock leading to *Sedgers Bank and Skysea*. See also *Culver Hole*.

SALTHOUSE POINT 1½ miles E of *Penclawdd* at *Crofty* near where the Morlais stream turns into Salthouse Pill, thence into the estuarine mud. **SS520956**

SAMSON'S JACK Massive (3.2 m high) standing stone W of *Oldwalls* in field S of Windmill Farm. FP access from Windmill Farm and from *Manselfold* Farm well worth a short expedition. **SS477923**

SANDS, THE Sandy inlet also known as *Slade Bay* in the rocky coast E of *Horton* reached by coastal FP from Horton or around point from *Oxwich*. **SS487854**

SANCTUARY Historic farmhouse near *Penrice* on lane leading to *Horton*. Once property of Knights of St John. The rather modern-looking house is said to incorporate fourteenth-century masonry. **SS488875**

SANDY LANE Unmade road linking *Southgate* to *Parkmill*. Now an area of chalet homes, and preferred location for artists and crafters. **SS548888**

SCURLAGE Village on the *Port Eynon* road (A4118), at the junction with the *Rhossili* road (B4247). During WWII the site was an American Army camp, due to the nearby beaches of *Oxwich*, *Port Eynon* and *Rhossili* resembling the beaches of Normandy; the lane down to Oxwich, off the A4118, is still known as the American Road. After D-Day the camp was used to house Italian prisoners of war. PH, shop, sports fields, holiday village.

½ mile nearer Swansea was a manor house, Scurlage Castle, built in fourteenth century by Sir Herbert Scurlage, who married into the Mansel family; now in private ownership. **SS463875**

SEDGERS BANK and **SKYSEA** Two protective ridges of sand and rocks below *Port Eynon Point*; accessible only along the shore. Both ridges become islands at spring tides and in stormy weather. Skysea was the site of the tragic wreck of the *Agnes Jack* in the worst gale Gower ever experienced (January 1883). The terrible loss of life led to introduction of a lifeboat at *Port Eynon*. The last member of the Lucas family to live at the *Salthouse*, the ruined house situated nearby on the coast, is reputed to be buried on Sedgers Bank. Skysea is a popular crabbing area. **SS473844**

SLADE Hamlet W of *Oxwich Green* which also includes the two farms of Western Slade and Eastern Slade. FPs from *Horton* (1 mile) and down the valley from E end of *Oxwich Green*. See *Sands, The*. **SS486858**

SLUXTON Remote Welsh long-house (dating to 18th century) farmhouse much altered, near Llangennith. Its origins might be linked to a faithful knight of Henry V, Sir Hortonk van Klux who took over Llangennith Priory *c* 1431-1435. **SS428897**

SMUGGLERS' LANE A track linking *Highway* Farm, home of the infamous smuggling Gower family, the Arthurs, to the secluded *Pwlldu Bay*.

SOUTHEND See *Oystermouth*.

SOUTHGATE Residential area within *Pennard*. A popular tourist destination with easy walks and fine view, plus coffee shops, restaurant and shop with PO. Bus terminus and CP (NT). PH and golf club at entrance to village.

FPs on cliffs (NT) to *Three Cliffs Bay* (1½ miles W) and *Hunts Bay* (1 mile E).

See *Foxhole*. **SS550880**

SPANIARD ROCKS Where the mainland juts out toward Burry Holms is a shelf of rocks with this curious name that may relate to a wreck. The W end of Gower is notorious for the number of wrecks that have occurred with much loss of life over the centuries. **SS403926**

SPRITSAIL TOR See *Prissen's Tor.*

ST PETER'S WELL See *Caswell Valley.* **SS594883**

STAFFAL HAEGR Modern and unusual spelling of what must once have been Ystafell Hagar. Former woollen factory along inland edge of marshes, ½ mile W of Llanrhidian. The Dix family operated the mill/factory throughout the nineteenth century until the looms were dismantled in 1904. Woollen blankets and carpets were made here. In its heyday the factory employed 6 to 8 people.
SS494926

STEMBRIDGE A large two-arched stone bridge carries the road from *Llanrhidian* to *Llangennith* over the Burry Stream. Nearby is site of former Stembridge Mill. Originally it was almost certainly a late medieval mill although precise documentary evidence does not exist until 1631. In the late nineteenth century the Dix family took it over and converted it into a woollen factory (see *Staffal Haegr*). The last weaver operated here until 1924. Stembridge Mill was one of the many mills along the Burry stream. Nearby there is a defended promontory fort possibly of Iron Age date. It may also be the site of a twelfth-century Norman timber Castle. In private ownership.

FPs to *Cheriton* across *Ryer's Down* and along valley.
SS468917

STONEMILL See *Parkmill.*

STOUTHALL (Formerly Stout Walls). Imposing country house, designed by Jernegan (1787-1790), in once elegant park, near junction of A4118 at *Knelston* with lane to *Reynoldston*. Originally the home of the influential Lucas family. Subsequently a maternity home and then a study centre for a London borough and currently an outdoor activity centre.

In a field opposite (E) was a pre-Norman pillar stone, found by a Lucas and erected here in early nineteenth century, some say over the grave of his horse.

The Stone is now in *Reynoldston* Church. The stone circle, a Lucas folly, which once stood in a field to W of lane (½ mile to NE of Stouthall), was removed in 1998. **SS475893**

Pillar stone when in situ at Stouthall

SWANSEA AIRPORT After passing through *Upper Killay*, Swansea Airport is the main feature to be seen on *Fairwood Common*. The airport was constructed during WWII as an RAF fighter station. Unfortunately, two Bronze Age barrows or burches had to be destroyed during its construction. Cinerary urn from one of the sites, Bishopston Burche, is in SM. Now used mainly for private and pleasure flights, flying school and sky-diving business. **SS565915**

SWANSEA (Welsh – **Abertawe**) Swansea is the chief town of Gower and has been since medieval times. With an estimated population of 245,500 (2017) it is the second largest centre in Wales and became a city in 1969. It has been much written about over the centuries and a detailed guide is beyond the capacity of this small guide. The visitor to Gower should not, however, be left ignorant of what the city has to offer; it is full of historic and visual interest together with all the attractions of an important regional centre. The Guide here offers ten worthwhile places in Swansea to visit.

1. **Swansea Marina** Based on the old South Dock of Swansea's once thriving coal and copper port. Here is found the National Waterfront Museum with extensive displays telling the story of the port and much more. Areas of attractive Georgian housing close by. Cafés and restaurants and home to the Dylan Thomas Theatre.

2. **Swansea Museum** Formerly the Royal

Institution of South Wales, Swansea's oldest museum (founded 1835) – Dylan Thomas said it should be in a museum – a distinctive and impressive building in its own right. Fascinating displays of local history and a centre of interest in Swansea's heritage.

3. Follow a **Dylan Thomas trail** – Dylan is, arguably, Swansea's most famous son and, by following one of the trails (available online), much can be learned about the poet, his art and the 'ugly, lovely town' that was his home.

4. Visit **Singleton Park** One of Swansea's and Wales's great urban parks. It occupies sloping, partially wooded land, given by the important Vivian family in the Sketty neighbourhood of the city. Splendid views of Swansea Bay, botanic gardens and buildings of great interest around the park. The Vivians' original house is now the administration block of Swansea University.

5. The **Glynn Vivian Art Gallery** Glendinning Moxham (1865-1946) was a Swansea architect of some renown – this is thought to be his masterpiece. The gallery has, in its collection, important paintings by Augustus & Gwen John and Ceri Richards, among others.

6. Take a **trip up the River Tawe** aboard the Swansea Community Boat – *Copper Jack* – from the South Dock and see something of 'Copperopolis'. Swansea was once the copper capital of the world.

7. The **Brangwyn Hall**, part of the Guildhall with its impressive clock tower at the W end of the city centre. An impressive building in its own right, this houses the huge Brangwyn Panels by Frank Brangwyn, originally intended for the House of Lords. In construction, the height of the walls of the hall had to be increased to accommodate the panels.

8. **Promenade along Swansea Bay** from the docks to the Cenotaph and beyond – see varied sculptures and Swansea Jack monument with fine sea views across the Bristol Channel.

9. **Medieval Swansea**. At the top of Wind Street are the remains of Swansea's castle; and nearby is the medieval Cross Keys Inn, still in use. Across the road is St Mary's Church – not medieval in build, but inside are some late medieval remains from the original church.

10. Visit **Swansea's Indoor Market**, the largest in Wales, in the city centre. An impressive space to be in; there is a great range of local produce (especially excellent fish counters) and local characters to be seen.

SWEYNE'S HOWES (or Swine Houses or Sweyn's Houses). Situated on E slopes of *Rhossili Down* are two Neolithic tombs. Tradition has it that this is the burial place of Sweyn, the Scandinavian sea-lord who may have given his name to Swansea (Sweyne's-ey). **SS422898**

TALBOT'S WAY See *Cefn Bryn*.

TALGARTH'S WELL An ancient well near *Middleton*. The water was highly prized for butter making due to its coldness. **SS428881**

TANKEYLAKE MOOR Open moorland between *Llangennith* and *Llanmadoc Hill.* Some stories retell a battle between inhabitants of *The Bulwark* and those at *Hardings Down* fort. The leader of the defeated Bulwarks was called Tonkin and it was said that the blood rose above the warriors' boots, hence Tankeylake. **SS434918**

TEARS POINT (NT) Headland to W of *Fall Bay*. **SS410870**

THE BEACON See *Rhossili*. **SS420888**

Arch at Three Cliffs Bay

THREE CLIFFS BAY Where Pennard Pill meets the sea. Together with *Worms Head*, Three Cliffs Bay is the most photographed area of Gower, if not S Wales. Sand dunes and salt marsh and the nature of the Three Cliffs formation disguise the dangerous currents in this bay, which make it unsafe for swimming and other water sports. Access by FP from *Parkmill* and *Southgate* plus by track including stepping stones up to *Penmaen*.

See *Pennard*. **SS536877**

THREE CROSSES (Y Crwys) An ancient way from the N of Gower crosses the old turnpike road from Swansea to *Penclawdd* and another way towards *Llanrhidian* via Welsh Moor: hence three crossroads. Other explanations of the name relate to a connection with Llangennith Priory and the existence of three crosses, but no supporting evidence has ever been found for this. Formerly scattered miners' cottages with some old farms such as Crwys and Killan. Three Crosses is now a large N Gower village, with a number of modern housing developments. The village is dominated by the large Capel y Crwys (1877) designed by John Humphrey of Morriston Tabernacle fame. The Welsh Independent chapel is associated also with the Prices of Cwrt y Carne on the *Loughor* estuary. Centre of the new Christmas Tree farm. Shop, PO, PH. See *Poundffald*. **SS569943**

THURBA (NT) Sometimes 'Thurba Head'. Impressive 70 m headland forming E side of *Mewslade* Bay. It was donated to the NT by Stephen Lee, one of the founder members of the Gower Society (see *Port Eynon Point*). Iron Age promontory fort. Accessible by foot from Great Pitton Farm, or by sheep track up from Mewslade Bay. Nearest parking: *Pitton* (very limited but field open for parking with honesty box). A small rocky inlet on E side of *Thurba* is known as *Butterslade*. *Ramsgrove* is a rocky pebble inlet W of *Paviland* and ½ mile E of *Thurba*. Winding inland is a fine slade, typical of Gower – broad, wild and craggy, with scree piled at foot of high bare cliffs. A landscape of glacial origin. **SS421868**

TOR BAY At E end of *Oxwich*

Bay. Popular sandy bay with steep approaches and with the dramatic pinnacle of the *Great Tor* on its E side. Accessible by FPs from *Penmaen* (1 mile). A large restored limekiln, one of many remnants of the once important lime industry in Gower, stands at the head of the bay. Other restored limekilns can be seen near *Kilvrough Manor*, in *Green Cwm*, and at *Landimore*. Lime burning was a significant industry in Gower between 1800 and 1960 but was past its peak by 1913. Small quarries and ruined kilns are still dotted around Gower; most were run by individual farmers to supply agricultural lime to their own and nearby farms. A commercial kiln operated at Hills near *Llanmadoc* until the 1930s and the kilns at Colts Hill, *Oystermouth*, were filled in during the early 1960s. Here the Norton Lime Works switched to making asphalt before eventually closing down in the 1970s. **SS528877**

TOWERS, THE On main south road (A4118). E gateway to Penrice Park, at junction with road down to *Oxwich*. The picturesque ruins of curtain wall of castle and drum tower are imitation, a nineteenth-century folly of the Talbot family, which was once used as a lodge and occupied by estate staff, now a holiday cottage. **SS502884**

TRINITY WELL See *Ilston Cwm*.

TRUMPET LANE See *Knelston*.

TUTT HEAD Small headland between *Limeslade Bay* and *Bracelet Bay*, formerly site of Coastguard Control Centre (closed 2015). **SS628871**

TWLC POINT Small, low limestone headland on W of *Broughton Bay*. Separates the wide expanse of Broughton Bay from the more intimate Little Broughton. **SS416932**

UPPER KILLAY Continues on from *Killay* (B4271), although originally part of *Bishopston* parish; here suburbia gives way to the open expanse of *Fairwood Common*. Cattle grids on road are to prevent sheep, cattle and ponies straying off the common. As on all Gower roads, take care to avoid the animals. **SS585927**

VENNAWAY LANE An early main road in Gower linking *Pennard* to the south road, and Fairwood common. Near the N end is a well preserved lime kiln near a former quarry, reminders of a once important industry. See *Tor Bay*. **SS564895**

VILE, THE Unique in Wales, a survival of a medieval open field system W of Rhossili. It forms part of the nationally important, registered historic landscape of W Gower. It is now owned and managed by NT. Variously spelt 'Viel', Vile' or Vyal' (pron vile). See *Rhossili*. **SS410875**

WALES COASTAL PATH A section of the national long-distance path traces the coastline around Gower from Loughor to Swansea Bay.

WALTERSTON Farm on N slopes of *Cefn Bryn* 1 mile NE of *Penmaen*. Once, with *Cillibion*, belonged to Neath Abbey. The remnants of the former hamlet of Walterston can still be seen near the farm. **SS515895**

WELSH MOOR Open moorland 1 mile E of *Llanrhidian*. The name is a reminder that this was a boundary in former times between Welsh Gower (*Gower Wallicana*) and English Gower (*Gower Anglicana*). A wild and beautiful stretch of common, it is an important habitat of the internationally rare marsh fritillary butterfly. **SS520925**

WEOBLEY CASTLE (Cadw) The 'castle' is, in fact, a well preserved later medieval fortified manor house, built by

the de la Bere family, probably on an earlier defended site. It is well fortified, but its crenelations and corbels are subordinate to its domestic arrangements. Its picture-book towers are slender and contain only stairways and latrines. Most of the surviving buildings were built in the early fourteenth century and are grouped around a courtyard. There is a simple gatehouse on the W, with private apartments for the lord of the castle between it and the spacious great hall on the N. Kitchens and service rooms stand on the E, and on the S is a room over which the castle chapel once stood. At the SW corner is the base of a massive square tower, probably pre-dating the manor house since its function appears to be seriously defensive. Until the fifteenth century the castle belonged to the de la Bere family. Later illustrious owners included Sir Rhys ap Thomas, the Herbert family and the Mansels. In about 1403, during Owain Glyndŵr's rising, the buildings were extensively damaged, but were soon repaired and in use again. From the seventeenth century the castle served as a farmhouse. In 1911, it was placed in the care of the State.

There are fine views across the Burry Estuary – at low-tide all sands and marsh. The tower at the end of the private concrete road out onto the marsh is the Spotting Tower used during the 1939-45 war when the area was a firing range.

See *Berthlwyd*. **SS479927**

WERNBWLL Above *Blue Anchor* where a large colliery was operated from *Berthlwyd* between 1893 and 1931. On 28th November 1929 seven men were killed in a gas explosion and the mine never really recovered. The site of the mine is marked with a memorial to the men killed and the area has been landscaped to include footpaths and a picnic spot with parking. **SS554947**

WERNFFRWD (Welsh – Gwernffrwd, alder stream). An old Welsh hamlet, first mentioned in the fourteenth century, near the Marsh Road between *Llanmorlais* and *Llanrhidian* at the edge of the Llanrhidian marshes. Originally a farming settlement, Wernffrwd became important for coal mining from about 1620 up to 1900. Also connected with the cockle industry. Nearby is the chapel formerly known as the St David's Mission Room, dedicated in 1898. **SS517941**

WERN-HALOG (Welsh – gwern, alder and halog, muddy). Formerly a farm of medieval origin between *Crofty* and *Llanrhidian*. Now adjacent to a large caravan site. **SS507932**

WERNLLATH Two farms, Upper and Lower, between *Clyne Common* and *Barland Common*. Formerly a Welsh-speaking hamlet of up to 12 houses and a pub called The Ivy Bush. Wernllath was a division in the parish of *Bishopston*. Licence was granted in 1672 for a Congregational Meeting House. Accessible via a FP from Barland Common. **SS588905**

WHITEFORD BURROWS and **SANDS** Wild expanse of dunes and pine plantations running N of *Llanmadoc* into the *Burry Estuary* (1½ miles) to Whiteford Point, where there is an old lighthouse, the only sea washed cast-iron lighthouse in UK (built 1865). Flanked on W by fine, secluded, two-mile sweep of Whiteford Sands. National Nature Reserve and NT property. Access by foot only. This is an area of exceptional natural interest and walkers are asked to keep to beach or FP.

See also *Berges Island*.
SS444945 – SS447966

WHITE MOOR site of former nineteenth-century woollen mill E of *Rhossili Down*. A wheel remains and traces of mill pond.
SS427902

WIDEGATE (pron Wijet) Isolated, ancient hamlet in Pennard parish, halfway down *Bishopston Valley*, never large but formerly having more dwellings. *Smugglers Lane* and old lanes to Hunts Farm, Hael, *Kittle, Backingstone* and *Pwlldu* converge here, ½ mile from St Mary's Church. Recorded since at least 1583, Edward Lluyd stated 'within this Parish stood Wydiat, some time ye house of Reinallt Jak, whose living was divided among his three daughters.' Part of the *Penrice* then *Kilvrough* estates until 1920. Lord Swansea lived here. Another cottage has a date stone 1771. **SS566881**

WORMS HEAD (OE – wurm, dragon). Locally known as The Worm. A mile-long serpent-like promontory at most W tip of peninsula. It is a tidal island, accessible for 2½ hours either side of low water. The crossing is over the Shipway or Causeway between the Inner Head and the mainland. The large anchor is all that is left of the Samuel, a Norwegian coal boat wrecked in 1884. Between

Middle and Outer Heads is a bridge of rock – Devil's Bridge. Along Outer Head is a blow hole, where air is forced through a cleft in the rock-face by wave action on N face of the Worm.

Devil's Bridge

A National Nature Reserve, fascinating in richness of flowers and sea-birds, which are protected and should be disturbed as little as possible. Visitors are requested to keep away from the outer parts between mid-March and July, when birds are nesting.

Warning. Before going out check time of tides and crossing times, displayed on boards at the Coastwatch at the top of the path going down to the crossing.

SS384877 – SS405872

YELLOW TOP See *Paviland Caves.*

ZOAR See *Crofty.*

Three Cliffs Bay

LANDSCAPE

South Gower cliffs: The Knave with Worms Head and Rhossili Down in the distance
Geraint Owen

The varied landscapes of Gower make a dramatic impact on visitors to Britain's first Area of Outstanding Natural Beauty. The most iconic are surely the rocky headlands and sandy bays of the south and west coasts, where cliffs line the edge of a plateau-like surface about 60 metres above sea level, on which sits inland Gower's patchwork of fields, hedgerows, woodland and villages. This surface is underlain by limestone, which formed on the sea floor some 350 million years ago, in the early Carboniferous period. Gower then resembled today's Bahamas, submerged beneath warm, clear, shallow seas in tropical latitudes. The sea bed was rich in invertebrate animals like corals, brachiopods (lamp shells), crinoids (sea lilies) and snails. Their shells remain as fossils, which can be seen as white markings in the grey rock. Over millions of years, layers of sea-bed sediment built up to a thickness of almost 1000 metres. They can be clearly seen in the south Gower cliffs. As older layers were buried, they hardened into rock: the Carboniferous Limestone. Over time, the sea varied in depth, storminess, clarity or the abundance of life, changing the characteristics of the rock. The limestone can be subdivided into units such as the High Tor Limestone, rich in fossils and exposed towards low tide at Three Cliffs Bay, and the Oxwich Head Limestone, exposed not only around Oxwich Head but also at Mumbles and Limeslade. Limestone slowly dissolves in weak acids in today's environment, forming underground caves and caverns, like those in Bishopston Valley.

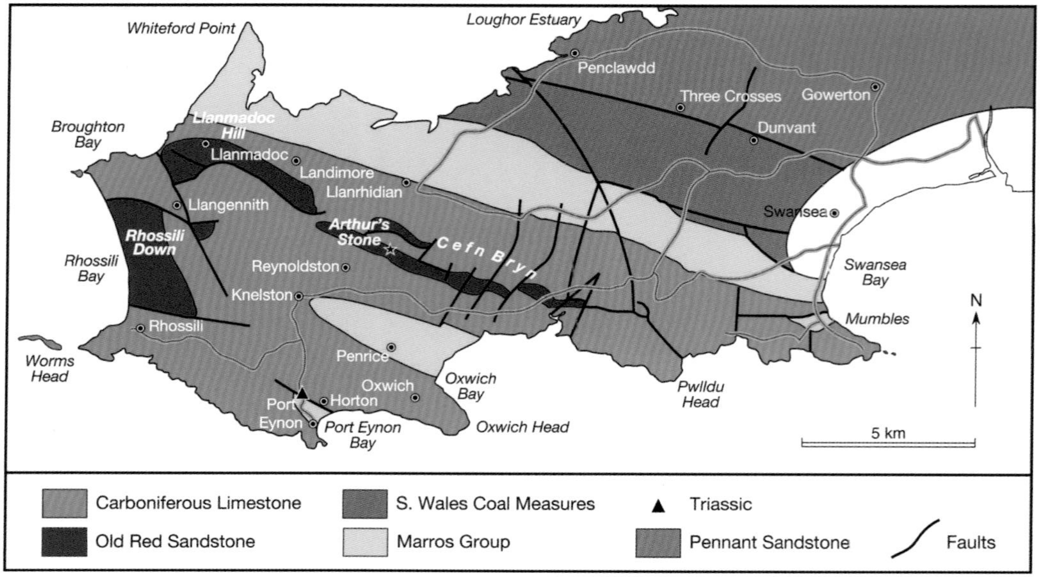

Geology of the Gower peninsula (from Shakesby R.A. and Hiemstra, J.F. (Eds), 2015. The Quaternary of Gower: field guide. Quaternary Research Association, London)

Rising above the limestone plateau, the hills of Cefn Bryn, Rhossili Down, Llanmadoc Hill, Ryer's Down and Hardings Down are open commons of rough grasses and heather. They are underlain by an older rock, the Old Red Sandstone, which formed about 400 million years ago, in the Devonian period. Rivers flowed from north to south across Gower, spreading sediment as they flooded. Sand, silt and gravel built up to over 1000 metres thick over several million years and hardened into sandstone, siltstone and conglomerate. Having formed on land, much of the rock is red and fossils are uncommon. Old Red Sandstone can be seen in small quarries scattered over the hillsides and in crags near their summits. Conglomerate with rounded pebbles of white quartz has been used in many buildings and walls and is known locally as the Pennard Conglomerate.

Except in the north and along Swansea Bay, few of Gower's settlements are coastal. The exceptions - Oystermouth, Oxwich and Port Eynon - lie at the head of broad, east-facing bays from which valleys run inland. The bays and valleys have been eroded along less resistant rock, the Bishopston Mudstones. These formed after the Carboniferous Limestone, about 320 million years ago, when fine mud settled to the floor of the shallow sea. They also underlie the boggy commons and moors of eastern Gower: Welsh Moor, Pengwern Common, Barland Common and Clyne Common. The rocks are poorly exposed but form the bed of the streams crossing Barland Common above Bishopston. Occasional layers are rich in small coiled shells of goniatites that swam in the muddy sea. Different goniatite species in each marine band are used to subdivide this part of geological time and, because of their importance, the Bishopston Mudstones on Barland Common are protected as a Site of Special Scientific Interest.

In the north-east of the peninsula, inland from Crofty, Penclawdd and Gowerton as far as Three Crosses, Dunvant and Killay, villages and towns are separated by rolling hills covered with a patchwork of small fields. This is part of the South Wales Coalfield, underlain by mudstone and sandstone interspersed with seams of coal, although little evidence remains of the mines that exploited this valuable resource. The Coal Measures formed late in the Carboniferous period, about 315 million years ago, when muddy deltas spread across south Wales. The area lay close to the equator, and the deltas were colonised by forests. Rotting vegetation in swampy pools was compressed first into peat and then coal. The Coal Measures are well over 1000 metres thick, although coal seams make up only a few percent of the total thickness. They can be examined on the West Cross foreshore and in overgrown cuttings and quarries along the Clyne Valley.

Much of ancient Gower lies north of the modern M4 motorway, taking in the high moorlands of Graig Fawr, Cefn Drum and Mynydd y Gwair to the north of Pontarddulais, Felindre and Clydach. This area is underlain by Pennant Sandstone, a thick succession of tough sandstones, again with seams of coal. The rocks accumulated when the deltas of the Coal Measures developed into rivers like today's Amazon. The remains of drift mines for coal can be seen along valley sides near the upper dam in the Lliw Valley and in the RSPB reserve at Cwm Clydach. Because of its toughness, Pennant Sandstone was quarried for walls and buildings in Swansea and neighbouring towns. Paving slabs of Pennant Sandstone, once very extensive, now remain in only a few areas such as parts of the Maritime Quarter and Mount Pleasant.

Between the Devonian period and the end of the Carboniferous period a pile of rocks over five km thick built up. At the end of the Carboniferous period this accumulation ended. Through the processes of plate tectonics, continents slowly move around the Earth's surface, occasionally colliding. The rocks at their edges are buckled, broken and pushed upwards to form mountains like the Alps and Himalayas. About 300 million years ago, separate continents containing northern Europe (including Gower) and southern Europe collided in the Variscan mountain-building episode. Gower was close enough to experience some of the consequences. The rock layers we see in cliffs, quarries and road cuttings are no longer horizontal, but are tilted, bent (folded) and broken (faulted). Layers tilted steeply to the north can be seen all along the south Gower cliffs from Rhossili to Port Eynon, while east of Horton they are tilted to the south. South of Oxwich they are tilted to the north. At Great Tor they are vertical. On the south side of Mumbles Head layers are tilted to the south and on the north side to the north. The rock layers on Gower are folded like a concertina. The mountains may once have been as high as the Alps but erosion has worn them down, cutting through the folded layers to reveal older rocks (Old Red Sandstone) in the centres of up-folds (anticlines) and younger rocks (Bishopston Mudstones) in the centres of down-folds (synclines). Because the Old Red Sandstone is more resistant to erosion than other rocks on Gower, the anticlines stand proud as hills, whereas Bishopston Mudstones in the synclines form valleys and bays. In between, the Carboniferous Limestone underlies the main plateau-like surface of Gower. Enhanced erosion along fractures and faults has formed smaller bays, such as Limeslade, Caswell, Three Cliffs and Mewslade, and explains the separation of the headland and tidal islands at Mumbles. On a larger scale, a major syncline extends from Gower northwards to the Brecon Beacons, with the youngest rocks of the Coal Measures and Pennant Sandstone in the centre; this is the South Wales Coalfield, which includes the north of Gower.

The Variscan mountains were probably worn down to sea level in a few tens of millions of years. For most of the time since then, the shape of Gower's land surface has changed little, although at times it was submerged beneath the sea. During the Triassic period, just over 200 million years ago, desert conditions prevailed across Britain. Red mudstone and sandstone were deposited on Gower, but have been almost completely removed by erosion apart from an area near Port Eynon once quarried as a pigment material. Rocks near today's land surface often have a red stain from the former Triassic cover. The stepped landscape, well seen from the south Gower cliffs, may have developed under those desert conditions, or perhaps through marine erosion as southern Britain underwent phases of uplift in the last ten to twenty million years.

Since about 2.6 million years ago, Earth has been in the grip of an ice age. Cold glacial episodes, when ice extended to temperate latitudes, have alternated many times with warmer interglacials like today, with ice confined to high latitudes and altitudes. The last interglacial was about 120,000 years ago. Sea level was higher than today, and cemented shelly gravels can be seen as raised beaches covering platforms about ten metres above today's sea level in places such as Rhossili, east of Horton, and Caswell. Then conditions got colder. Relatives of today's hippos, elephants and hyenas that lived on Gower in the interglacial were replaced by mammoths and reindeer. Their bones and teeth have been found in some south Gower caves. Human remains have also been found, notably the Paviland burial, discovered in 1823 and dating to about 30,000 years ago. Glaciers reached their maximum extent some 20,000 years ago, when most of Britain was covered by an ice sheet like the one in Greenland today. Its southern limit straddled Gower; north Gower was glaciated, but south Gower was not. Because so much water was locked up as ice, sea level was more than 120 metres lower than it is today; the Bristol Channel was a marshy, midge-infested river plain. Glaciers and ice streams gouged steep-sided, flat-floored valleys like the Swansea and Loughor valleys. Meltwater near their edges carved the Clyne and Bishopston valleys and the slades of south-west Gower. And when the ice melted away it left a veneer of deposits across the landscape, called till. This includes erratic pebbles and boulders from as far away as north Wales and southern Scotland.

For about the last 11,700 years - the Holocene epoch - climate and vegetation have gradually changed to what we know today. As ice melted, sea level rose, driving ahead of it sand that had been deposited on the floor of the Bristol Channel by meltwater, to form sandy bays fringed by sand dunes. Before the sea reached its present level, woodland had covered the coastal plain and the remains of tree stumps, logs, roots and occasional deer antlers can be found in the submerged forests of Swansea Bay and Broughton Bay. Finally, people left their marks on the landscape in the form of buildings, roads, fields and caravan parks: the story of a changing landscape continues.

Geraint Owen

BEGINNINGS

Arthur's Stone

When the first evidence of people in Gower appeared, the last great ice ages were still to come. Mammoth, bison and reindeer survived in large numbers. The human population of Britain consisted of only a few scattered communities, relying for life on the animals they could hunt and the berries and plants they could gather. Flint tools made by these Palæolithic people have been found in several of the Gower caves, including Paviland and Longhole. When these caves were occupied, the Bristol Channel was a wide river valley, and the caves faced south across it. In Paviland Cave, some time around 30,000 BC, the skeleton of a young man was buried with the skull of a mammoth at his feet and trinkets of bone about him. It was excavated in 1823 and, because the bones were thought to be of a female and were stained red with ochre, it became known as the Red Lady of Paviland. These bones are now in the University Museum at Oxford, and the Bristol Channel floods above his hunting ground. It is one of the oldest examples of a ritual burial in western Europe.

The food-gathering life of these people persisted with little change for many thousands of years, but a slow increase in technical skills is indicated by discoveries of small, skilfully-worked flints on open sites such as Burry Holms, Llangennith, which may have been occupied about 10,000 BC. Evidence for occupation during the Mesolithic period (c. 10,000 BC – 4,000 BC) has also been found at other sites such as Cat Hole. The land in upland Gower was poorer and it does not seem as if it was much occupied during that time.

The beginning of the Neolithic period (c. 4,000 BC - 2,000 BC) is marked by agriculture becoming a basis for life. Chambered tombs were constructed by the peoples of this time, apparently for communal use. Two forms of these tombs are found in Gower. The most impressive of these is Arthur's Stone on the high ridge of Cefn Bryn. A 25-ton capstone still roofs the burial chamber and the whole structure was once covered with a mound. On the eastern slopes of Rhossili Down stand Sweyne's Howes, two smaller tombs of similar type and date to Arthur's Stone. On Penmaen Burrows, half-buried in the dunes, there is a more complex tomb of the same period. This tomb has a stone-lined entrance passage and a side chamber opening off the central area. The capstone of this tomb weighs seven tons. Parc-le-Breos burial chamber, also known as the Giant's Grave, is a chambered tomb with a forecourt leading to a central passage, off which were side chambers. It was restored after an excavation in 1960 and is one of six of this type found on Gower.

Soon after 2,000 BC the use of copper, and in due course, bronze was introduced into Britain by people from north-west Europe. These newcomers did not practise communal burial, but buried their dead singly beneath large earth or stone mounds, cremation becoming more frequent in later periods of the Bronze Age (c. 2,000 BC – 600 BC). Copper and bronze daggers and well-made pottery frequently accompanied the deceased in their last resting places. The edges of these burial mounds were often reused for burials later in this period. A fine Bronze Age mound can be seen near the main road at Cillibion (half-a-mile west of the road junction). Two other similar mounds were destroyed by the construction of Fairwood Airfield. In upland Gower, Mynydd Pysgodlyn round barrows and Penlle'r Bebyll ring cairn are among several Bronze Age sites accessible to the public.

The Iron Age (c. 600 BC – 43 AD) is represented in Gower by over 30 sites. Hill forts characterise the settlements. Cilifor hill fort is the finest in Gower, and consists of three great ramparts and ditches enclosing a steep-sided hill. Other impressive fortifications are to be found on Harding's Down, the Knave at Rhossili and The Bulwark on Llanmadoc Hill. These substantial hill forts may have had several purposes – for defence, or meetings and markets, as religious centres or perhaps tribal gatherings. As well as the large hill forts there are many smaller enclosures and promontory forts in the peninsula particularly along the south coast which are probably the remains of small hamlets or farms defended by banks and ditches for some small protection in troubled times.

The Bulwark, Llanmadoc Hill looking west Jeremy R Douglas-Jones

Our knowledge of prehistoric life depends on the skills of archaeologists. However during the later Iron Age the expanding Roman civilisation reached Britain, and from this time written records give some assistance. References to Britain by Roman writers are few and references to Wales fewer. But the Roman invasion of south Wales around 47 AD marks the start of our history.

When the Roman forces arrived in south Wales the strongest tribe among the Iron Age peoples here was the Silures – Gower was towards the western edge of their territory. Fierce resistance from them between 47 AD and about 79 AD delayed the Roman conquest of south Wales, but by the later date the Romans had established a pattern of military roads and forts which held Wales more or less under Roman rule for more than 300 years. Gower settlements in the peninsula probably changed little but north of this the area may have been more affected. A road from the east ran through Neath (called Nidum by the Romans) then to Loughor (Leucarum) and on to Carmarthen (Moridunum). The Roman fort at Loughor lies below the medieval castle and the A484. It was extensively excavated in the 1980s. A Roman building stood at Oystermouth, where fragments of mosaic are on view in the church, and, above the quarry at Barland, Bishopston, Roman pottery, glass, charcoal and ironwork indicate that a settlement stood nearby in the 2nd century AD. There is evidence too of a major Romano-British site near Church Hill, Ilston. Military practice camps were constructed on Carn Goch and Stafford Commons. Roman material including pottery and coins has been found around Gower - some is on display in Swansea Museum.

When, in about 400 AD, the Roman military finally abandoned Britain, south Wales reverted to the old Iron Age pattern of small independent kingdoms. Through these, the great saints of the Celtic church, Dewi, Teilo and Cadog, spread the Christian faith, and several of the Gower churches are dedicated to them. At Llanmadoc church a Christian tombstone survives from about 500 AD, and at Swansea Museum there is a Roman altar from Loughor which was reused as a tombstone at the same date. Llangennith was the site of a small Celtic monastery founded by St Cenydd in the 6th century, but destroyed by Viking raiders.

In the 11th century, the Normans found independent Welsh states or kingdoms. These were soon overrun by Norman lords, whose king allowed them to hold their conquests as Marcher Lordships, with powers approaching those of autonomous rulers. Soon after 1100, Gower had been annexed and had become a Norman Marcher Lordship, with the new town of Swansea as its fortress and capital. The Norman possession of Gower was neither undisputed nor secure, and successive attempts were made by the rulers of the Welsh states of Cardigan and the Vale of Towy to dislodge the invaders. At least six times between 1113 and 1217 the Welsh burned castles in Gower and devastated the countryside. The castles which bore the brunt of this fighting were constructed of turf and timber with earth and rubble defences - Penlle'r Castell on Mynydd y Gwair at the very north end of the Lordship of Gower was maybe one of these border fortresses designed to warn of Welsh attacks. But from the later 12th century stone defences were added, becoming, by the end of the 13th century, the robust structures typified by the castles of Oystermouth, Pennard and Penrice among others. Although some were damaged during Owain Glyndwr's revolt between 1400 and 1413, the construction of these stone castles marked the failure of Welsh resistance.

One result of the conquest was that Gower was thrown open to settlers from the West Country, and it is to the influx of English people at this time and to the subsequent cross-channel traffic that the distinctive character of the people and the peninsula is due. The medieval system of open-field cultivation was practised extensively in the peninsula, and at Rhossili is one of the few remaining medieval strip field systems in Britain, known as The Vile (locally spelt Viel). Small settlements formed around the early medieval churches replacing the scattered Welsh farms. The manorial system in the peninsula was Norman but in the parts of the Lordship north of Swansea, the old Welsh landholdings survived into the 18th century.

Within the peninsula, the limit of English colonisation appears to be defined by the belt of open moor formed by Clyne, Fairwood and Pengwern Commons, and by Welsh Moor. North of this line the population was, and is, largely Welsh in origin and outlook. This is the poorer land where the coal measures outcrop, and here, from the 16th century coal was worked and exported. At Penclawdd the only industrial centre in the peninsula was established, and from the 18th century the brass, copper, lead and coal industries brought prosperity to the area. Coal was mined in the north-east of peninsular Gower until the 1950s.

Away from the Penclawdd area, industry in Gower was limited to the extensive quarrying and processing of limestone, much of which was shipped to north Devon. The limestone industry was very active during the 19th century, and many of the derelict coastal quarries and kilns can be found. Oyster fishing was another important 19th century occupation and the remains of the perches, or storage pools, can still be seen at Port Eynon and Mumbles. Overfishing of oysters by the 1870s and 1880s left many families destitute.

The area close to and north of Swansea became highly industrialised between the later 18th and early 20th centuries. It had coal and wealthy local entrepreneurs willing to exploit it. Improvements to the port provided good transport links, and in the 19th century Swansea became a world centre for tinplate and zinc production and smelted 90 percent of the world's copper, earning it the name 'Copperopolis'. The town expanded but industry caused huge pollution problems leaving the Swansea Valley one of the largest areas of industrial dereliction in western Europe. Since the 1960s, however, the Lower Swansea Valley Project has worked to reclaim the land.

Today, most of the industry has disappeared. Leisure and tourism are of far greater importance – golf courses and caravan parks are the major users of land apart from the agriculture that still survives as it has done since the first immigrant farmers erected Arthur's Stone so many years ago.

Jane Sherrard-Smith after Bernard Morris

Cilifor Top

CASTLES

Oystermouth Castle

The Lordship of Gower (Gŵyr), the largest pre-Norman *commote* in Wales, was created around 1106 when Henry I gave the area to his close friend and ally Henry de Beaumont, Earl of Warwick. The defence of the newly-acquired land was maintained by the construction of castles, of which about twenty are currently known. These castles are a significant group in Wales, being densely sited and displaying most of the key features in the development of the castle as a medieval fortress in the two hundred years from the arrival of the Normans to the late 13th century. They also give a rare insight into how the Normans settled, parcelled out and altered the landscape of Gower.

The location of these castles is significant. The main castle, the *caput* of the Lordship, was at Swansea, taking advantage of a riverine location with good access to the sea. Two castles, Loughor itself and Llandeilo Talybont, near Pontarddulais, were built on the banks of the river Loughor in order to control access into the Lordship from the west. To the south, the major castles of Oystermouth and Pennard were kept in the possession of the chief lord for his own use and financial benefit. Further west, a string of castles, such as Penmaen, Mountyborough (Penrice village) and Norton, were constructed along the south coast of Gower, taking advantage of the good agricultural land. These castles were constructed by the followers or knights of the Earl, with one family, de Penres, taking its name from the Welsh area Pen-rhys, which today survives as Penrice. The stone-built and impressive Penrice Castle replaced the original castle at Mountyborough and was built on a new site. Other castles, such as Cilifor Top, built within a pre-Roman Iron Age hillfort, were constructed on the north of the Gower peninsula to protect the area from Welsh attacks. Later in the Middle Ages, with the defence of the lordship against major Welsh assaults becoming a serious issue, the new stone castle of Penlle'r Castell was constructed on the northern border of the Lordship on Mynydd y Gwair in the earlier 13th century.

The earliest castles in Gower were built in timber. They were strongly built fortifications, which, apart from the construction material used, would not have been dissimilar in appearance to the stone fortifications that immediately succeeded them. These timber fortifications took two forms – the familiar motte and bailey and the ringwork castles. Of these two types, the ringwork is by far the more common in Gower with only two certain mottes, built at Loughor and Llandeilo Talybont, both significantly built on the western border of the Lordship. The motte is a large, man-made, conical mound on which was built a timber stockade surrounding a two-or-three-storey timber tower or keep. This was the key defensive structure and final refuge in the event of the castle being overrun by attackers. Below the motte a defended enclosure or bailey, housing the main castle buildings, such as halls, granaries, stables for the knights' horses, blacksmith, kitchens, chapel, etc was constructed. The ringwork, having no adjacent motte, took the form of a bailey enclosure, with the strongpoint being the tall timber gatehouse/keep. All timber castles were defended by deep ditches and strong earth ramparts, on which were built solid timber walls with fighting platforms and towers. For reasons still not completely understood, ringworks predominate in Gower, a good and accessible example being Penmaen Castle, overlooking Three Cliffs Bay.

Over time these timber castles, which were vulnerable to fire attack, were strengthened with stone fortifications, mainly with stone curtain walls and square or rectangular stone keeps as the main defence. A good example of this 12th century progressive castle design and development is Oystermouth Castle. During the 12th and into the 13th centuries new ideas of castle fortification were brought back by the crusaders from the Middle East. They included stronger curtain walls with mural towers, round stone keeps replacing the earlier squared forms, and gatehouses with twin drum towers on either side of a defended gate passage comprising strong timber gates and portcullises. Good examples of gatehouses, which had now developed into the strongest defensive component of castles, can be seen at Oystermouth and Pennard castles.

The great stone castles of the later 13th century, such as Caerphilly in south Wales and the north Wales castles of Edward I, such as Harlech, mark the pinnacle of castle building in Britain. A decline in castle building, for many reasons, followed with greater emphasis being given to comfort and improved living space over military necessity. Gower has three fine examples of this later form of fortified manor house, namely Swansea New Castle, Weobley and Oxwich castles, all of which can be visited.

Much more research needs to be given to the Gower castles as an important national collection in the landscape – why so many were built, why they were built in their locations, by whom and why the ringwork form of timber castle was mainly chosen by the early castle builders. We also need to know why so many of the timber castles were not refortified in stone and, as it seems, went out of use in the early thirteenth century, after only a hundred years or so of service.

The castles of Gower are an important collection of medieval fortifications and are places of insight into the Middle Ages, as well as inspiration and enjoyment today. The following sites are recommended for visits, being open to the public or accessible. Further brief information on individual sites is provided in the gazetteer.

Timber motte castle – Loughor Castle.

Timber ringwork castle – Penmaen Castle; Cilifor Top

Early 12th century stone tower and later development – Oystermouth and Weobley Castles

Early 13th century stone castle – Penlle'r Castell

Later 13th century stone tower – Loughor Castle

Later 13th century stone twin-towered gateways – Oystermouth and Pennard Castles

Later 14th-16th century manorial fortifications – Swansea, Weobley and Oxwich castles

Other castles are in private ownership and permission to access them should be obtained from the owners. Many, however, can be viewed from a distance or from public footpaths.

Charles Hill

Aerial view of Penrice Castle. The image is Crown copyright and is reproduced with the permission of Royal Commission on the Ancient and Historical Monuments of Wales (RCAHMW), under delegated authority from The Keeper of Public Records.

CHURCHES

St Cadog's Church, Cheriton

One of the glories of Gower is the presence of a number of medieval churches. Some of these buildings have enormous charm, others are of architectural distinction, all are of interest. The Christian Church has been present in Gower, more or less continuously, for somewhere around fifteen centuries; the ancient parish churches of this region are a direct link with the earlier churches of this area. Many of the buildings are probably located on the same site as their early predecessors and some contain carved stones attesting to the antiquity of the Christian tradition there. Although the buildings themselves are ancient (generally about 700 years old), the sculptured or lettered stones are even older and date from the Celtic Church period (the Church before the introduction of the medieval Roman Church), their ages ranging from 800 to 1,500 years. A number of sixth century records in the Book of Llandaff concern 'Llans' in Gower, some of which can still be positively identified.

In medieval days only three churches were under lay control, whilst the remainder were under ecclesiastical rule, split between monastic, episcopal and university ownership. After the dissolution of the monasteries some of the churches in monastic ownership passed to either lay impropriators or were retained by the Crown. This state of affairs ended in 1923 when the Church in Wales was disestablished and became a separate Province within the Anglican Communion.

It is not often realised that the number of medieval churches in Gower today is only about one half of those that are known to have existed. Among the ruined churches is the only site in Wales where direct evidence for a wooden church from the Celtic Church period has been found – this is Burry Holms chapel. Although it is the ancient parish churches which automatically spring to mind, Gower has a ruined chapel in Ilston Cwm, reputed to be the first Baptist meeting place in Wales, near the site of a pre-Reformation chapel.

Until recent times Gower was a relatively remote area and its churches do not display the splendour often found in other regions. This area was never wealthy and, as the Anglican Church in Wales lost its revenues on disendowment, the Gower churches are now dependent upon donations by parishioners and visitors for building preservation.

Finally, the churches and their early monuments constitute a rare continuum of visual evidence spanning over 1,500 years of Christianity. Most of the ancient stones are with their associated churches. However, the Roman altar from Loughor, with its Ogham (early Irish) writing, and the Gellionen Stone are in Swansea Museum.

The parish churches are :-
Bishopston (Llandeilo Ferwallt – St Teilo)
Cheriton – (St Cadog)
Ilston (Llanilltyd Gyr – St Illtyd)
Llandeilo Talybont (St Teilo, now at St Fagans National Museum of History.)
Llandewi (St David)
Llangennith – (St Cenydd)
Llangiwg (St Ciwg – now privately owned)
Llangyfelach (St David and Cyfelach)
Llanmadoc – (St Madoc)
Llanrhidian – (St Rhidian and St Illtyd)
Llansamlet (St Samlet)
Loughor – (St Michael)
Nicholaston – (St Nicholas)
Oxwich – (St Illtyd)

Oystermouth – (All Saints)
Penclawdd – (St Gwynour)
Penmaen – (St John the Baptist)
Pennard – (St Mary)
Penrice – (St Andrew)
Port Eynon – (St Cattwg)
Reynoldston – (St George)
Rhossili – (St Mary)
St John juxta Swansea

Llangiwg Church Rod Cooper

Window at St Mary's Church, Rhossili

Graveyard at St Illtyd's, Ilston

CHAPELS

Bethesda Chapel, Burry Green

The everyday meaning of the word 'chapel' is of a nonconformist building for Christian worship, while a church, particularly in Wales, means an Anglican or Roman Catholic place of worship (even though these may contain side, or other, chapels).

Nonconformist congregations are 'gathered church', rather than congregations that assemble on a parochial basis. In chapels it is the pulpit rather than the altar in a central position from the congregation's view point, for chapels were primarily built as places of preaching, having a communion table rather than an altar, and with minimum ritual or ceremonial. Before chapels were built, worship at places other than those of the Established Church took place in cottages and farmhouses, often in conditions of secrecy. The farmhouse of Cwm-mawr near Three Crosses was used for this purpose in the 17th century, and it became licensed as a place of worship after the 1689 Act of Toleration had eased the situation for nonconformists. The meetings at Cwm-mawr developed to the extent that a Welsh congregational chapel was erected at Three Crosses in 1788 and this was enlarged on the adjoining plot to Capel y Crwys in 1877. Gower's first chapel for dissenters (who after the 1662 Third Act of Uniformity can also be termed nonconformists) was also the first Baptist chapel in Wales, at Trinity Well in the Ilston valley. This was erected on land owned by Rowland Dawkin of Kilvrough, after the Restoration of the Monarchy in1660 had led to Revd John Myles being ejected from the living at Ilston. The Baptist cause, which he pioneered in Wales, waned when the legislation of the 1662 Act made it untenable to continue his ministry in Gower, and particularly once he had emigrated with several of his congregation to North America. Ten years later in Rhossili, the home of one Richard Bevan was licensed as an Independent meeting house, and by 1676 they had a congregation of 45 – about a third of the population of the parish. The fact that the Welsh Methodist leader, Howell Harris, chose to visit Rhossili in May 1742 indicates that a group of dissenters continued to meet in that area. After the Wesleyan Methodists seceded from the Anglican church in 1759, purpose-built chapels began to appear and this escalated with the establishment of the Calvinistic Methodists as a separate denomination in 1811. The Baptist movement also began to establish places of worship; as early as 1807 a chapel was built above Crofty, 'Mount Hermon', as a deliberate attempt to oppose the secularisation of this industrial part of Gower.

Diana, Baroness Barham, visited Gower and was so moved by 'the darkness of the place and the spiritual destruction of its people' that she moved to Gower (Fairyhill) in 1814. Before her death ten years later, Lady Barham had built six Calvinistic Methodist chapels. Religious revivals, as in Pembrokeshire in 1806 and national ones as in 1859 and 1904, contributed to a rapid growth in nonconformity. Besides the primary usage of the chapels as places of worship, they were used for educational purposes, especially as Sunday Schools. Capel Isaac in Blue Anchor (Penclawdd) may have been used only as a schoolroom, rather than for any Sunday worship.

A feature often adopted in chapel design that distinguished the buildings from places for other uses was round-headed windows, often of double height. Larger chapels in the industrial areas of 'Welsh' Gower – Bethel and Tabernacle in Penclawdd and Capel y Crwys in Three Crosses – have a gallery encircling all four sides with a large pipe organ in the gallery behind the pulpit whilst Trinity, Penclawdd, has a gallery on three sides. English chapel designs predominate in the peninsula's rural areas with no galleries apart from Bethesda, Burry Green, a rear and side gallery, and at Murton

Methodist a recently-added rear gallery.

Within a decade of the 1904-05 Welsh Religious Revival, the number of chapels in use in peninsular Gower reached a peak of 35; but the twentieth century brought the carnage of two World Wars which, allied to the effects of liberal theology, undermined the faith of many. Furthermore, the advent of radio and television contributed to chapels ceasing to be social centres of the community. By 2007 the number of chapels in use had fallen to 23, the same figure as in 1851 when a religious census was taken in Wales,.

The non-conformist chapels of Gower are numerous, many of them are referred to in the gazetteer and some deserve special note. A few are particularly worth noting and these have additional notes in the gazetteer.

Bethesda in Burry Green
The first Baptist church in Wales in the Ilston valley
Paraclete chapel in Newton
Bethel chapel in Penclawdd
Reynoldston Methodist chapel

The notes above, together with the entries in the gazetteer relating to the churches, are by local historians Luke Toft and Gary Gregor.

Carmel Chapel, Cilionen

CROSSES IN GOWER

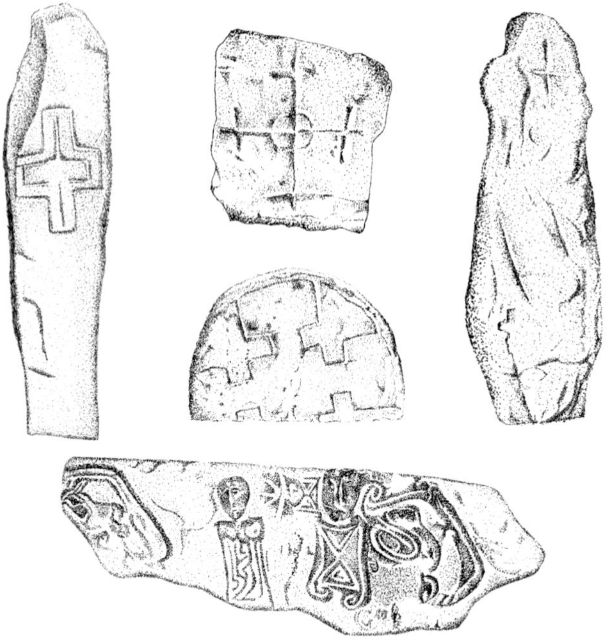

Ancient Stones of Gower – associated with Gower churches.
Top left - Pillar Cross, Reynoldston c. 9th century
Centre top - Boundary stone, Llanmadoc c. 13th century
Top right - Pillar cross, Llangennith , early medieval
Centre - Wheel cross, Llangiwg c. 9th century
Bottom - The 'Leper' Stone, Llanrhidian, enigmatic stone, date surmised c. 9th – 10th century

These are examples listed by L A Toft in his article on Celtic Church monuments in the Gower Journal (Gower 35 – 1984). He also notes more stones of interest at Gelli-onnen, Llangennith, Llangyfelach, Llanmadoc, Loughor, and Reynoldston. Some of these stones are now in Swansea Museum.

Art work – Rod Cooper

DIALECT

Members of Bishopston manor court outside the Valley Hotel, 1920s

Like south Pembrokeshire, Gower has had an English-speaking population for many centuries. Due to its isolation, surrounded on all sides by areas where Welsh was spoken, a distinctive dialect developed with a depth and richness that is all but lost. If you hear it today, it will be a few words here and there, but within living memory there were people whose language was rich with words and turns of phrase, delivered in a lilting accent that sounded more West Country than Welsh, but with a music all its own.

It caught the attention of several writers over the years, many of whom include a brief glossary of words that took their fancy. The earliest was Isaac Hamon, who wrote a report on Gower for the historian Edward Lhuyd in 1697. He lists 46 words and some phrases, and states "the southern part, about Oxwich, Penrees, Porthynon and all the parishes in that parts, did pronounce their words something like the West of England, as v instead of f, or z for s, and the like, and the Northern part about Llanridian, Cheriton etc they pronounced likewise, … but they inclined more to the Welsh, and mixed some Welsh words amongst their old English." Other useful sources include the Rev. J. D. Davies in his four-volume book *History of West Gower* (1877-1897), and C. D. Morgan, *Wanderings in Gower*, published in 1886.

The glossaries they compiled were not scholarly or systematic, and many of the old words inevitably died out without being written down. We are fortunate to have some invaluable recordings of Gower folk made in the 1960s and 1970s that give us the chance to hear their speech in all its richness. These can be accessed at West Glamorgan Archives. Gower dialect finally received academic scrutiny in *Gowerland* and its Language by Rob Penhallurick (1994), reissued in précis form as *The Gower Glossary* by Benjamin Jones and Rob Penhallurick, 2018 (available online at www.swansea.gov.uk/article/46601).

Horatio Tucker, writing in 1950, said "The next few decades will most certainly see the complete eclipse of dialect speech in Gower." Like Isaac Hamon, he noticed many elements of West Country dialect, fostered by centuries of trade between Gower and north Devon, in words like 'blonkers', 'bet' and 'nestletrip'. The meaning of these words is given in the glossary below.

The relative isolation of English-speaking Gower meant that some words and phrases, such as 'charnel' and 'rying', were retained long after they became obsolete elsewhere. Other words, such as 'nice', 'melted', 'frightened' and 'starved', retained their original meaning while modern usage has moved on.

Not surprisingly, the Gower dialect absorbed plenty of Welsh words as well. Horatio Tucker quotes the examples of 'bubback', 'glaster' and 'carthen'. He notes that there were regional differences across the peninsula, some words even being limited to parochial usage. An example of the latter is the word 'bumbagus', used at Oxwich as a name for the bittern, which was formerly found on the marshes there. Local variation in words is illustrated by the word 'frawst', which, in one particular parish was pronounced 'froist'. There were also two words for cockchafer – 'dumbledarey' and 'oakwib'. The former word was the older and could be found throughout the peninsula, while 'oakwib' was met with only in south Gower, probably having been introduced by Devon settlers during the heyday of the limestone trade.

Horatio Tucker finishes with a typical example of Gower speech as told to him by an old Gower sailor, who related the story of an incident from his youth, in Port o' Spain, Trinidad, in the 1880s:

"Me an' Davy Hoskin tuck ah turn out o' th' town t' zee how th' zhuggar was ah-kerning, an' when we was ah-coming back drow th' town, ah vella come out o' ah drangway, – just like that there! an' ah lucked at me, quite noppit like, and ah zed – "Be you one o' th' Bennons o' Partennan?" an' I zed, "Aye, that I be," an' I lucked at he, zz'snow, an' I zed "An' who art thee?" an' ah zed "I be one o' th' Griffies avram Langeny," an', zz'snow, thee cust ha' knocked me down wi' ah veather.

"Davy – he was ah herrin'-gutted zort o' vella wi' ah leery belly – zo th' dree of us makth vor th' ship an' hath ah dobbin o' rum an' ah lil froist, an' we never wanted no cuzzenin', I can tell thee. An', zz'snow, I nivver zeed ere ah zign o' Tom Griffy, – only once, – in Port Elizabeth. I zed t' un then, me an' Davy 'ud take ah turn t' Langenny, zumtime, but there 'tis, as 'tis, Davy bin gone an' I'th ah nivver bin there ite, an' I don't 'spose I 'ull now, 'vrall, – come t' my years. I'th ah bin t' mill t' Stembridge, many ah time, an' t' Lamaddock, t' Mapsant, but Langenny be ah furrin' country t' me. Mabbe them "Oxen" 'uddent fancy ah "Crow" rhining around, v'rall."

DIALECT

The following glossary of words occurring in the text is typical of Gower dialect words once in common usage.

bett, prepared turf used for hedging.
blonkers, sparks.
bubback, scarecrow, also a dull person.
bumbagus, the bittern.
carthen, a winnowing sheet.
charnel, a box-like space formed by raising the ceiling above the fireplace, for hanging bacon.
Crow, native of Porteynon Parish.
cust, could.
cuzzening, coaxing.
dree, three.
drangway, a narrow lane or alleyway.
drow, through.
dobbin, a large mug.
dumbledarey, cockchafer.
frawst, froist, a dainty meal.
frightened, astonished.
glaster, buttermilk in the churn.
herring-gutted, lean.
inklemaker, a busy person.
ite, yet.
jorum, a large quantity or helping of tea or beer.

keek, to peep.
kerning, ripening, also to turn sour.
leery, empty.
makth, makes
melted, broken up or disintegrated.
mucka, a rickyard.
nestletrip, the smallest pig in a litter.
nice, fastidious.
nipparty, perky.
noppit, perky.
oakwib, cockchafer.
Oxen, natives of Llangennith.
rining, mooching or scrounging.
rying, fishing.
scrabble, to gather up hastily objects on the ground, e.g. children scrambling for money thrown to them.
starved, perished with cold.
tite, to overturn.
uddent, wouldn't.
v'rall, for all.
zz'snow, do you know.

Andrew Dulley, after Horatio Tucker

PLACE-NAMES IN GOWER

Here are some of the most common elements found in Gower place-names. Note that in Welsh, adjectives come after the noun:

aber, mouth of river, confluence. W.
afon, river. W.
allt, gallt, hillside. W.
bach, fach, little. W.
bryn, hill, mound. W.
burrows, sand-hills, dunes. O.E. *beorg*, hill, mound.
cae, field. W.
canol, ganol, middle. W.
carn, cairn, heap of stones. W.
castell, castle. W.
cefn, ridge. W.
cil, nook, shelter, retreat. W.
clawdd, hedge, ditch, bank. W.
clyne, meadow. W. *clun*.
coch, goch, red. W.
coed, wood. W.
craig, graig, rock, crag. W.
cwm, valley. W.
down, hill. O.E. *dun*.
du, black. W.
ffald, pound. W.
ffrwd, stream. W.
furze, gorse bushes. O.E. *fyrs*.
gate, gap, gate, passage, road. O.E. geat, a gate; O.N. *gata*, a road.
gelli, grove of trees. W.
glais, lais, stream. W.
gors, cors, bog, fen. W.
gwern, wern, swamp; alder

trees. W.
gwyn, wen, white. W.
hayes, hedge, enclosure. O.E. *hæg*.
hen, old. W.
heol, road. W.
hir, long. W.
hole, cave. O.E. *hal*, a secret place.
holm, island. O.N. *holmr*.
isaf, lower
knap, knab, top, summit. O.E. cnæpp.
lake, stream. O.E. *lacu*.
lang, long. O.E.
ley, woodland clearing. O.E. *leah*.
llan, enclosure, church. W.
llech, flat stone, slab. W.
llwyn, grove, bush. W.
llys, court, palace. W.
maen, stone. W
mawr, fawr, big. W.
melin, felin, mill. W.
mere, pool. O.E.
môr, sea. W.
morfa, marsh, fen. W.
mynydd, mountain. W.
nant, stream. W.
newydd, new. W.
onnen, ash tree
parc, park, field. W.
pen, top, head, end. W.
pentre, village. W.
pill, tidal creek. O.E. *pyll*.
pont, bont, bridge. W.
pwll, pool. W.
rhos, moor. W.
rhyd, ford. W.
sker, reef, rock. O.N.
slade, dry coastal ravine. O.E. *slæd*.
tir, land. W.
ton, enclosure, farm, village. O.E. *tun*.
tor, crag, rock. O.E. *torr*.
tre, tref, town. W.
tŷ, house. W.
uchaf, upper. W.
waun, gwaun, moor. W.
way, path, road. O.E. *weg*
wich, farmstead, dwelling place. O.E. *wic*.
worm, serpent, dragon. O.E. *wyrm*, O.N. *ormr*.
ynys, island, river meadow. W.

O.E., Old English; O.N., Old Norse; W., Welsh

Pill Cottage, Llanmadoc

THE COMMONS

Fairwood Common

The common lands of the Gower peninsula are so extensive that they represent an exceptional survival of a medieval landscape. Common land covers approximately twenty percent of the area of the Gower Area of Outstanding Natural Beauty. Some of these commons probably go back to prehistoric times when the better land was used for arable crops and the more distant, less fertile land used for communal pasture for livestock. There were few inhabitants, so there was little need to define these areas exactly or the inhabitants' rights. As populations increased there was a need to limit usage of these communal areas; even before the Norman Conquest there was the beginning of definite ownership of these lands and of certain rights granted to the local farmers.

After the Norman conquest of Gower, the land was held by the Marcher Lord or Lord Seigneur, whose vassals held small manors. These vassals, in turn, sublet lands within those manors to tenant farmers and freeholders. The land was farmed on classic manorial lines, with arable strip fields and communal grazing on the unenclosed poorer uplands, cliffs, marsh and heath. These grazing lands were manorial waste or commons; adjacent tenant farmers and freeholders were the commoners. They had *rights of pasture* (grazing of livestock), estover (use of small branches and underwood, including bracken taken to provide bedding for the animals in winter), *turbary* (digging of turf or peat for fuel in their dwelling), *piscary* (fishing) and *coire* (use of surface stone on their holding).

Gower generally escaped the great enclosure movements of the 18th and 19th centuries. This was partly because some commons were poorly drained and unsuitable for agricultural development, but mostly because of the management policies of the Duke of Beaufort and the Penrice Estate, the two major landowners at that time. This may have been because both concentrated their efforts in exploiting the minerals to the east and north of Swansea. Port Eynon Moor was a notable exception, as it was enclosed in the late 17th century. There was also a small amount of encroachment onto common land by squatters and farmers especially after 1650. Farms were small, with low investment (tractors only came to Gower in 1934) and the landscape changed little.

The major use by the commoners of Gower was for grazing and each commoner had a 'stint' which allowed him a certain number of stock that could be grazed, depending on the size of his holding. In Gower, approximately one and a half acres of holding entitled the commoner to graze one beast or pony, or alternatively five ewes with lambs. Many farms depended on this right for economic survival. Intercommoning rights allow animals to move between adjacent commons. The other rights occasionally exercised nowadays in Gower are *estover* and *coire*, but the taking of surface stone or gravel may conflict with present planning legislation, or be contrary to SSSI designation.

Today, there are around 500 commoners in Gower, while the major landowners are the Duke of Beaufort (Somerset Trust), National Trust, the City and County of Swansea, and Llangennith Manors Ltd (a company formed by the commoners of Llangennith and Llanmadoc to purchase the freehold of their own commons). The Penrice Estate has sold most of the common land it had previously owned to National Trust.

The commoners formed the Gower Commoners Association in 1947 to represent their interests. When the Commons Registration Act of 1965 was introduced by Parliament to resolve the many difficulties and interpretations over commons ownership and usage following the abolition of manorial system of management in 1922, they registered all their grazing lands and interests. Other areas of land have been registered in accordance with the provisions of the 1965 Act on the basis that they are 'manorial waste' – the open, uncultivated and unoccupied 'lands of the manor'.

Usage of some commons has decreased due to a number of factors, some practical such as young farmers not wanting to undertake the hard work involved in tending animals grazing on the commons, and changing of farming practices. Other factors are the social/economic changes of farming and living patterns, including the speed of motor vehicles on the roads crossing the commons causing accidents involving animals, so that the economic loss of valuable stock cannot be sustained by the farm owner. The reduced grazing has led to deterioration of the vegetation (*e.g.* grass replaced by bracken, gorse and scrub).

Fencing and/or cattle grids to prevent animals straying off commons have been of enormous help, but such schemes are expensive. Unless carefully designed they can spoil the open aspect that the commons give to Gower. However it may be considerably better to contain animals and encourage grazing, rather than allow grazing to finish and the commons to rapidly 'scrub up' and became impenetrable jungles. Traffic calming measures within commons would be beneficial. Scrub clearance is a continuing issue.

Since 2000 the public have had legal rights of access over all commons except for areas of golf courses and other areas as defined by Schedule 1 of the Countryside and Rights of Way Act 2000.

A representative few of these commons are considered in more detail below. Their diverse flora and fauna are described elsewhere in this Guide. Many of the commons are, or contain, Sites of Special Scientific Interest (SSSIs). There is additional information in the Gazetteer for specific localities such as Cefn Bryn.

Salt Marsh – Llanrhidian and Landimore Marshes

These salt marshes have been used for common land grazing for hundreds of years. A survey of Gower Anglicana in 1583 states: 'The lord and tennants of this Lordship may enter all commons as Llanrhidian Marsh and any other and have done tyme out of minde, without contradiction as farre as we know without lett or

Commons, the AONB, National Trust land and the Gower Way

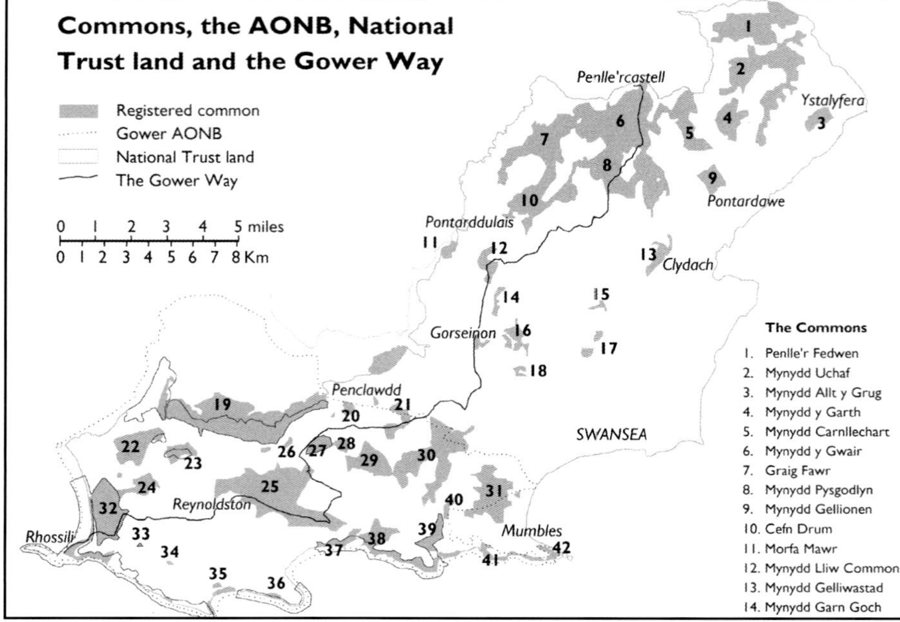

The Commons

1. Penlle'r Fedwen
2. Mynydd Uchaf
3. Mynydd Allt y Grug
4. Mynydd y Garth
5. Mynydd Carnllechart
6. Mynydd y Gwair
7. Graig Fawr
8. Mynydd Pysgodlyn
9. Mynydd Gellionen
10. Cefn Drum
11. Morfa Mawr
12. Mynydd Lliw Common
13. Mynydd Gelliwastad
14. Mynydd Garn Goch
15. Llangyfelach Common
16. Stafford Common
17. Mynydd Bach & Mynydd Cadle
18. Mynydd Bach y Glo
19. Llanrhidian Marsh
20. The Wern & Rallt
21. Mynydd Bach y Cocs
22. Llanmadoc Hill
23. Ryers Down
24. Harding's Down
25. Cefn Bryn Common
26. Cilifor Top
27. Welsh Moor
28. Forest Common
29. Pengwern Common
30. Fairwood Common
31. Clyne Common
32. Rhossili Down & Cliffs
33. Pitton Cross
34. Pilton Green
35. Port Eynon Point & Sedgers Bank
36. Horton & Slade Cliffs
37. Nicholaston & Penmaen Burrows
38. Pennard Cliffs & Burrows
39. Bishopston Valley
40. Barlands Common
41. Newton & Langland Cliffs
42. Mumbles Hill

interruption'. This is one of the largest commons on the Gower peninsula with an area of 1531 acres, belonging jointly to National Trust and the Somerset Trust. The salt marsh is regularly washed by high tides, and the commoners graze sheep and ponies together with a few cattle. Salt marsh-grazed lamb is now marketed as a local speciality.

Ponies usually walk in with the tide, although they will sometimes remain standing in the rising tide on slightly higher ground and wait till the tide recedes; under modern legislation this age-old habit now causes animal welfare concerns. Sheep do not move in with the tide, so have to be brought in by the flock master or they will drown. All animals including those turned out on common land have to be ear-tagged or chipped for animal health regulations.

The marsh has a very characteristic flora, including cord grass, which was introduced to the area in 1935 to control erosion and trap silt. Cord-grass is also grazed by ponies. The Burry Inlet, of which this marsh is a part, has an exceptional range of bird life. This has led to its designation as a renowned Ramsar site. The marsh is also used for cockle gathering; there have been cockle pickers since the earliest times (see the Gazetteer entry for Loughor River).

Inland Commons – Welsh Moor, Fairwood and Clyne Commons

The soil of these commons is acidic, mostly glacial drift on Millstone Grit with many poorly drained areas. Welsh Moor is notable for the marsh fritillary butterfly, whose caterpillars feed on the devil's bit scabious. Fairwood was donated to the Swansea County Borough in 1935 by Arthur Owen Thomas, lord of the Manor of Pennard, as successor to the Kilvrough Estate, with rights of general access. An aerodrome was constructed on it during WWII. Many tons of hardcore had to be used on the boggy areas for this purpose and, unfortunately, two Bronze Age cairns or 'burches' were destroyed. Clyne Common, being an urban common, has a general right of usage by the public for 'air and exercise' and also has a golf course. Fencing of roads and installation of cattle grids have helped to improve conditions for grazing animals and thus improve the common itself.

Upland Peninsular Commons – Rhossili Down, Llanmadoc Down, Hardings Down and Ryer's Down all fall into the same group as Cefn Bryn and have many similarities.

Cefn Bryn is the largest single common in peninsular Gower with an area of 2041 acres. It is owned by the Somerset Trust, the Penrice Estate and National Trust. It contains the second highest point in peninsular Gower as well as Arthur's Stone, a Neolithic tomb, and many other Bronze Age remains. The ridge is of Old Red Sandstone giving an acid soil with fescue grass and bracken. The lower northern slopes are rather waterlogged in parts and there are many bowl-shaped depressions or sinks, a result of the collapse of caverns in the underlying limestone. Some of these sinks are water-filled as they are clogged with glacial clay and form small pools. The largest of these is Broad Pool, a nature reserve with interesting flowers, insects and birds. There is also a very large dry sink, Moormills, into which several small streams enter and disappear.

Grazing rights are recorded in the 1583 survey of Gower Anglicana, and the encroachment by two smallholders onto the common lands of Cefn Bryn is also mentioned. The right to 'cut furze and ferne for time out of mind' by the tenants of Walterston manor is given in a survey of 1689. Sheep, cattle and ponies still graze the common today, but not as many as earlier because of problems referred to before. As a result, the pasture in places is deteriorating. (See also the Gazetteer entry for Cefn Bryn.)

Sea Cliff Commons – Pennard Cliffs, Rhossili Cliffs, Pennard, Penmaen Burrows

These are all on the south coast of Gower, where the tops of the dramatic Carboniferous Limestone cliffs are covered by thin, well-drained soils. Many areas are covered by windblown sand from the great storms of the 14th -16th centuries, forming extensive dunes or burrows. Most of this area is owned by National Trust, but Pennard Burrows belongs to Pennard Golf Club. Ponies and cattle graze the inland, besanded area of Pennard, which is now grass-covered and a popular golf course. The cliff-top pastures adjoin the expanded residential areas of Southgate and the cliffs of Pennard – cattle grazing on the cliffs create ideal habitat for the chough – a success story of re-colonization of the Gower cliffs. But cattle create muddy walk areas and manure, or enter residents' gardens if gates are left open, which modern commuters seem to begrudge! Rabbits, probably introduced by the Normans, were farmed in artificial warrens now called pillow mounds, and provided fresh meat in winter. Such a mound can be seen on Penmaen Burrows near the old castle.

The many and varied commons of Gower will hopefully continue to serve, inspire, educate and interest local inhabitants and visitors alike for many generations to come.

Albert White and Edward Harris.

Broad Pool

Oak, Lower Lliw reservoir

Spindle, Bishopston Valley

FLOWERS AND TREES

Towards Millwood

Gower owes much of its designation as the first AONB in 1956 to its indigenous flora and fauna. It is an area of subtle contrasts – a microcosm of diverse environmental types. Here, you will find moorland, heath, farmland, cliffs, sand dunes, pebble and sandy beaches, woodland, fresh-water and estuarine habitats. In a short article, it is impossible to list every plant you can find – this is just a 'taster' to the enormous variety to be found.

A comparatively small area of Gower (some seven percent) is woodland, dominated by oak and ash, with some wych elm and sycamore but beech is not widespread; in Bishopston Valley, you can find the uncommon small four-leafed lime. The under-storey is likely to support holly, hawthorn, spindle, field maple, hazel and dogwood. Damp areas on commons will have birch; Oxwich has numerous alders and willow. Trees in Parkmill are excellent testimony to the pollution-free air, as they sport extensive lichen growth. Spring sees the woodland floor covered with dog's mercury followed by wild garlic (or ramsons), primrose, violet, bluebell, bugle and wood anemone. This is a scenic and scented splendour of riches, amongst which you may spot red campion, enchanter's nightshade, herb bennet, wood sanicle and daffodil (in some cases, the double form). Many woods hold stands of the bushy butcher's broom, where 'leaves' are actually side branches, and true leaves are tiny scales. It has inconspicuous greenish flowers on the 'leaves' which are followed by red berries – both may be present together. The diligent searcher may find toxic herb paris, pale chlorophyll-free parasitic toothwort (a member of the broomrape family), early purple orchid, stinking hellebore, Welsh poppy, and both caper and wood spurge. Common polypody fern is abundant on trees; it also grows on the ground. Ferns thrive in shady moist areas. The stinking iris (smell its leaves where they are damaged) grows beneath the pines on the sandy ground at Whiteford.

Coastal areas are subjected to salt-laden air and strong westerly winds which the plants have to tolerate. Trees show characteristic 'wind pruning' where exposed. Coastal grassland has spring squill, orchids, dovesfoot cranesbill and wood sage. Isle of Man cabbage and sea bindweed can be found behind Pobbles beach in the valley. Gorse and blackthorn are typical scrub plants amongst foxglove, salad burnet and carline thistle. Common and hoary rock rose, rock sea spurrey, wild thyme and basil thyme, common milkwort (pink, blue and white forms), devil's-bit scabious, and scarlet pimpernel (blue, red and pink forms) jostle for supremacy. On the headlands, those with a keen eye can locate diminutive autumn lady's tresses. Vertical rock faces may have the Gower speciality, yellow whitlow grass (easily seen on Pennard castle), wall pellitory, wall saxifrage and scurvy grass species. Beneath the cliffs and above the shore, you can find sea beet, golden samphire and rock samphire.

Yellow Whitlow grass (*Draba aizoides*) Ruth Ridge

The dune systems can be extensive. Oxwich and Whiteford have creeping willow with its frothy seed heads, wild privet, dewberry, burnet rose (which may have galls of the gall wasp) and stands of hemp agrimony, so beloved by insects. Isolated pines and yews are self-sown, and there are some established birch spinneys. Oxwich has an extensive sward of red campion, bluebell and cowslip in Spring – an inspiring sight. In recent years, grazing has effectively curtailed scrub development in some areas, allowing ground flora to flourish. Dune edges on the seaward side are dominated by the sand-consolidating marram grass. Further inland, biting stonecrop carpets its yellow swathes, together with wild thyme, bloody cranesbill, rest harrow (some may have white flowers), sea centaury, bird's foot trefoil, yellow rattle, yellow-wort, red bartsia, with viper's bugloss, sea holly, some bee orchids, evening primrose and pyramidal orchids. In the damper dune slacks, there is creeping variegated horsetail, early marsh and southern marsh orchid, common twayblade, marsh helleborine, marsh pennywort, and round-leaved wintergreen. The sight of the dune (Welsh) gentian thrusting from the sand is one not to be missed in late summer. At Whiteford, you can search for the rare and diminutive fen orchid. In the dunes, you may also spot the peculiar saprophytic, strikingly yellow-coloured yellow birdsnest. Oxwich has a large area of reedswamp, fen and willow carr, where you can find yellow iris, ragged robin, purple loosestrife, marsh cinquefoil, marsh bedstraw, water lilies, bulrush, common reed, reedmace, common sedge and water dock. The water also holds the insectivorous bladderwort.

Broad Pool, near Cillibion, has fringed water lily – a yellow delight in summer. Ponds and damper areas can also show, in and around their margins, extensive flora, such as broad-leaved pondweed, water starwort, purple loosestrife, angelica, toxic hemlock water-dropwort, water mint, brooklime, water forget-me-not, water bistort, water crowfoot (both large-flowered and ivy-leaved), common fleabane, spiked water milfoil, giant horsetail and sometimes bogbean.

The northern salt marsh has short-cropped, extensively-grazed vegetation, which in early autumn is a purple haze due to sea lavender. The flora can include sea plantain, sea rush, thrift, spear-leaved orache, sea mayweed, red fescue, buck's horn plantain and sea wormwood; in drier areas, yellow horned poppy grows. Edible salicornia (glasswort) is well worth a nibble! Below Llanmadoc, there is abundant yellow iris and marsh mallow. Cord-grass (*Spartina townsendii*) continues its stealthy advance, notably in Swansea Bay.

Commons cover large areas of Gower and, at first glance, may appear to be bracken-covered only, but they repay closer scrutiny. In the wetter parts, you will find cotton grass, common rush, cross-leaved heath, the insectivorous sundew, bog asphodel with its bright golden starry flowers and marsh marigold; elsewhere, there is gorse, lousewort, tormentil, delicate pale pink bog pimpernel, marsh St John's wort, lesser skullcap, fragrant meadowsweet, and cuckoo flower. The royal fern is rarer and there are excellent specimens between Sluxton and Llangennith. Upland areas, on the moist peat, have heather and bilberry but tend to be dominated by purple moor grass. Pink-flowered English stonecrop flourishes on the drier rocky areas.

Farmland can still produce corn marigold (Paviland area), field pansies and common spotted orchids (Henllys area). Arable weeds such as ramping and common fumitory, corn spurrey, field bindweed, groundsel, numerous thistle species, scentless mayweed, eyebright and silverweed often edge the crops. Dry-stone walls support numerous lichens plus the ubiquitous wall pennywort, ivy-leaved toadflax, dwarf maidenhair spleenwort, various cranesbill species, and rue-leaved saxifrage. Hedge banks, away from council-manicured verges, support colourful successive populations including the herb, majoram, field scabious, blue meadow cranesbill, Jack-by-the-hedge, wild arum, coltsfoot, greater stitchwort, hedge parsley all topped by clematis, honeysuckle, black bryony and dog rose.

No attempt has been made to deal in detail with the non-flowering plants which form such a vital, but less attention-stealing, part of Gower's rich floral tapestry (both on the shore and inland).

Ruth Ridge

East from Home Farm, Penrice

Three lifeboat stations and the lighthouse at Mumbles

SEASHORE LIFE AND TIDES

Cockle Shells, Oxwich Bay

There are a few different types of shore around the Gower peninsula, each with a different seashore community. On the north coast is the flat muddy estuarine shore of the Llwchwr (Loughor) river, and some of its tributaries such as the Burry. On the north-west coast and parts of the south coast are the sandy beaches so popular with visitors and locals alike. At the top of many sandy shores are sand dunes, with a vast array of flowers and other plants. On the west and other parts of the south coast are rocky shores and limestone cliffs, most of which rise to 60 metres (200 feet) above sea level. Many sea birds and cliff-dwelling birds nest on these. The rocky shores are the best for studying seashore life, since there is no sand or mud in which the animals can hide.

The rise and fall of the tides around the Gower coast varies considerably. Indeed, the Bristol Channel has the second highest tidal amplitude in the world. The spring tides are the ones with the greatest amplitude or range – the highest high tides and the lowest low tides. During the spring tides, the tidal range is sometimes over ten metres (33 feet). During the neap tides the range is a lot less. We are lucky in that the spring tides around the Gower coast have the low water at 12.00 to 2.00 o'clock (night and day) – and this is the time to be at the bottom of the shore looking for all the wildlife.

Neap tides have their low-water at about 6.00 to 8.00 o'clock. Always check local tide times when venturing below high water mark.

(The numbers in brackets in the following paragraphs are a reference to drawings by Gwen Thomas within this article.)

Seaweeds grow on the rocky shores. They are algae, and do not have roots, so they cannot grow in sand or mud. There are three groups of seaweeds – green, brown and red. Most grow in well defined zones on the shore. Of the green algae, the one at the top of the shore, and around freshwater runoffs, is gutweed (1). Sea lettuce (2) lives in the middle to lower shore, and is often abundant in rock pools. The dense tufts of fine green, wiry branched threads in some pools is Cladophora (3). The most obvious zonation is shown by the brown algae. The narrow-fronded, leathery channelled wrack is found highest on the shore, above the line of high-water neap tides. At and below high-water neap is the spiral wrack, the one with the swollen tips that look like heat-sealed polythene bags. Next down the shore comes the bladder wrack (4), with its air-filled floats in pairs. At mid-tide level and below we get either saw wrack, or, on very sheltered shores, the knotted wrack (5), which has single air bladders. At low-water spring tides we have the kelps or oarweeds. One of them, the sugar kelp (8), looks like a strip of puckered ribbon tapering to a root-like holdfast. Two other common ones, tangle and cuvie, have flat, broad blades, torn into strips by the action of the waves. Many beautiful red seaweeds grow in the rock pools, or on the rocks lower down the shore. There is the succulent pepper dulse (7), leaf-like dulse (9), feathery Ceramium (6), jointed coral weed (10), and crinkly forked Irish (Carrageen) moss, a source of agar (11). The laverbread for sale in Swansea Market is made from a red alga, laver weed (Porphyra). This grows at and above mid-tide level, a very thin, almost black or dark purple membrane lying on the rocks and stones. Seaweeds collected for mounting on paper should be kept in water and carefully floated on to the surface of the immersed paper. When dry they should be covered with transparent film or paper.

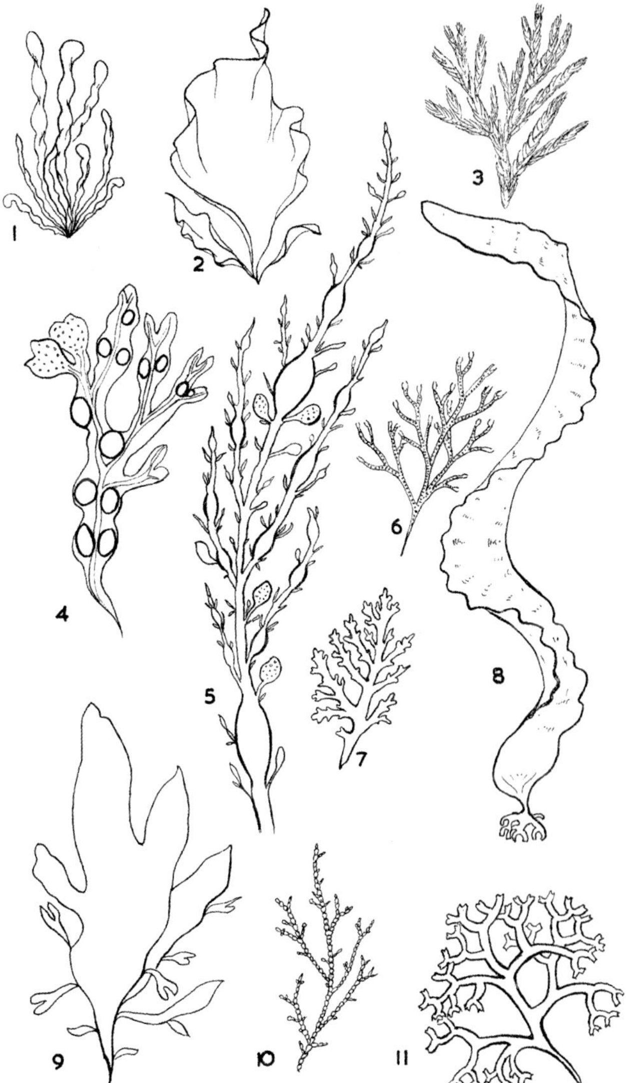
1
2
3
4
5
6
7
8
9
10
11

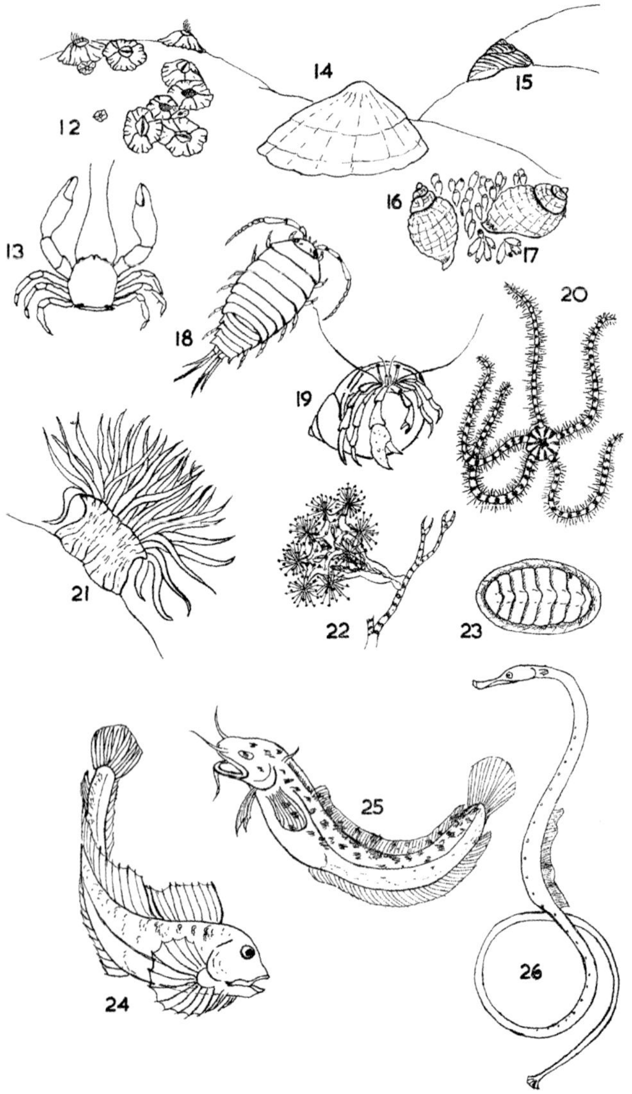
12
14
15
16
17
13
18
20
19
21
22
23
25
24
26

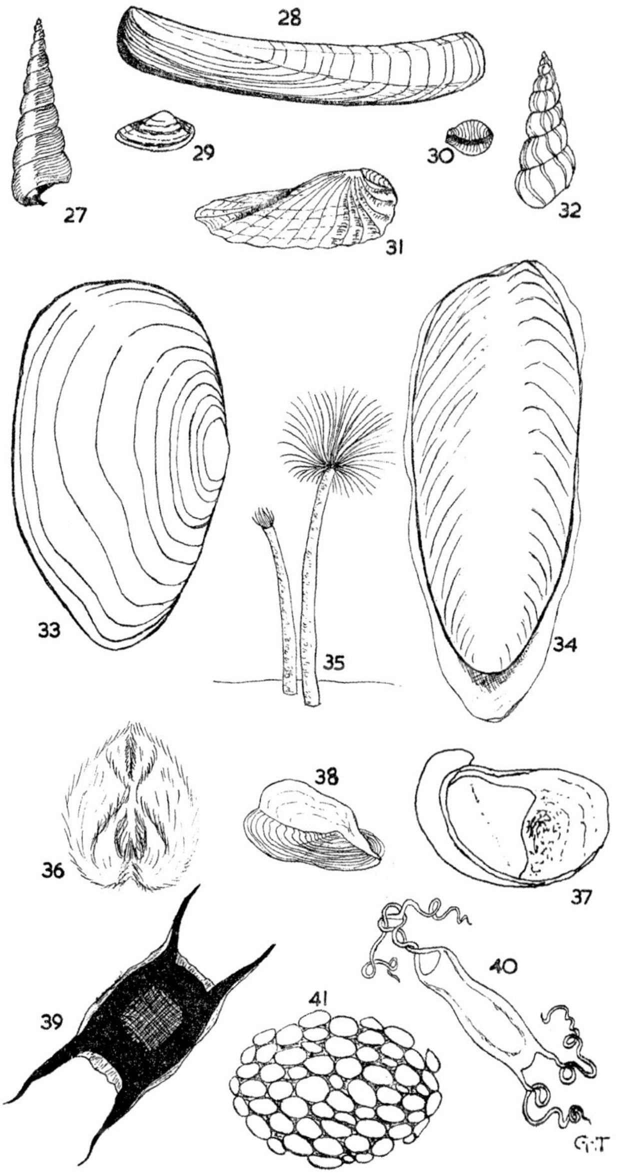
28
27
29
30
32
31
33
35
34
38
36
37
40
41
39
G.T

Animals on the seashore are varied and diverse. The shore is a very difficult environment in which to live, so the animals are all extremely well adapted to this, and no other, area.

Beginning with rocky shores, the rocks themselves are encrusted with acorn barnacles (12), especially higher on the shore. These are crustaceans, related to crabs and shrimps, but live a sedentary adult life in small conical shells cemented to the rock surface. Scurrying across the dry rocks at the top of the shore are sea slaters (18), the largest British woodlouse. Also on the rocks and in crevices may be found various molluscs which are relatives of the snail: limpets (14), periwinkles of all sizes and top shells (15) are all herbivores, feeding on the algae on the rocks when the tide is in. Dog whelks (16) are carnivores which feed on other molluscs and acorn barnacles; their cream or purple egg cases (17) are frequently found in clusters on the underside of rocks. Attached to the rocks by threads of protein are purple-blue mussels. These are bivalve molluscs, related to the cockle. Adhering to the rocks is another type of mollusc, the chitons (23), which are often mistaken for fossil woodlice. Below mid-tide level, there are a number of species of sponge growing. The most abundant on the exposed rock surfaces is the breadcrumb sponge, a creamy orange or pale green colour.

Around the edges of rock pools is a different, bright species, *Hymeniacidon*. In the middle shore, where sand is carried amongst the boulders and rocks, you may find a mass of honeycomb-like tubes of the reef worm. They make their tubes by sticking sand grains together. Wriggling along the rock surface, often amongst the barnacles, is the greenleaf worm; distinctively bright green. Under stones, especially in fine-grain sand, we sometimes find the ragworm, a whitish-pink colour, with its red dorsal blood vessel showing through its skin. Also under stones may be found various brittle stars (20), related to the common starfish (which is not a seashore species – those found on the shore are usually weakened and dying). Special to the Causeway at Worms Head are cushion stars - *Asterina phylactica*.

In rock pools you will find crustaceans such as prawns and hermit crabs (19) which use the shells of molluscs as a home. Under stones are other crustaceans such as the green shore crab, the pink edible crab and the very fierce blue and red fiddler or velvet crab, which has very flattened back legs. Young specimens are able to use these legs to swim. Low on the shore you will find the small broad-clawed porcelain crab, which is covered in hairs, and the even smaller long-clawed porcelain crab (13), which often pushes itself along backwards with its long claws. All crustaceans periodically moult their outside skeleton in order to grow, and seek shelter during this process. They are soft and very vulnerable until their new, larger, skeleton has hardened.

Attached to the rocks are several types of sea anemone. The blobs of red or greenish jelly on the exposed rocks are the beadlet anemone – they open to reveal a circle of tentacles when under water. In pools you may well see iridescent green or dull-red snakelocks anemones (21). These have tentacles so long that they cannot withdraw them. Distantly related to the anemones is the stalked jellyfish (22), which is usually attached to seaweeds, and very difficult to see.

The rockpool fish include the blenny (24), the bullhead, with a large head and spines on its gills, the rocklings (25), with barbels around their mouths, and the pipefish (26), which is common, but often overlooked since it resembles a strand of sea weed.

Broughton Bay

The magnificent sandy beaches such as Swansea, Oxwich, Port Eynon, Rhossili and the mud flats of the Burry Estuary, harbour a flourishing population of burrowing animals. Bivalve molluscs are numerous, and include razor shells (28), cockles and venus shells. Other bivalve shells will be found washed up on the strand line, including small tellin and wedge shells (29), and larger gapers (33), scallops and oysters. The fragile white piddock (31) will be found on some strand lines. Snail-type shells to seek include the cowries

(30), large polished necklace shells, pink and white-striped acteons, pointed tower shells (27), the ribbed spiral white wendletraps (32), and the slipper limpet (37), which was introduced from America, and resembles a Chinese slipper. A number of worms live in the sand, including the large greenish-black lugworm, often sought as bait, which throws up a coil of worm-like cast on the surface of the sand. The sand mason worm makes a tube by sticking sand grains and bits of shell together. The top of the tube is a fluffy fringe, and sticks up proud of the sand surface. The peacock worm (35) builds its tube from mud, and is only exposed by very low tides. When they are submerged, the worm pushes out a beautiful array of tentacles to trap food particles from the water.

Washed up after storms you may find several kinds of jellyfish, and the by-the-wind sailor (38), with its beautiful violet oval membrane under a curved fin-like sail. Occasionally one sees the deadly Portuguese man-of-war, (a close relative of the jellyfish) with its iridescent inflated sail. The test (outer skeleton) of the sea potato (36), which is a species of sea urchin, is often found; it is very delicate and breaks easily. The horny black egg cases of the skate (39) and the softer translucent ones of the dogfish (40) are sometimes found. These are both called mermaid's purses. Oval pieces of white substance, hard on one side with soft lamellae on the other are the cuttle-bones (34), the internal 'shells' of cuttlefish. These are collected to give to pet canaries and budgerigars which eat them to supplement the calcium in their diet. Loose balls of a membranous bubble-like material are the egg cases of the whelk (41).

Good hunting! However, a few words of advice: don't try to take fish or other animals home in jars, unless you have a seawater aquarium ready to receive them; they are not easy to keep. Also, after you have turned a stone over, please return it carefully, the right way up. There are many animals (some too small to see) which are living under the stone which will die if they are left exposed to the atmosphere. Tide tables can be purchased in a number of fishing and sports shops. They are also published in the local paper (the *South Wales Evening Post*). These give the times of high tides. Add six hours and ten minutes to estimate the time of low water. Aim to be on the shore before low water, and work your way down, to be at the tide's edge at the time of low water. That way you will see the animals and plants of the various levels of the shore – and I repeat, please return the stones carefully after you have upturned them.

Michael Isaac and Gwen Thomas

Whiteford Lighthouse

Beach huts at Langland Bay

Goose barnacles at Langland Bay

MARINE ANIMALS

Common Dolphins Mike Tonge

The most prominent marine mammals are Gower's Atlantic grey seals, which can be seen in ones and twos almost anywhere between Swansea Docks and Rhossili, usually off rocks. Numbers at the Worm are highest from June to August. They can be seen north of the inner head and in the rocky bay north of the Causeway. Some haul out soon after the flood and spend an entire tide idly on the rocks before lowering themselves back into the water at the next high tide. As many as fifty of these curious and unthreatening animals provide one of Gower's most memorable wildlife spectacles. There are no beaches suitable for the cows to calve and it is thought that calving, in late summer, is at Lundy and Caldey. Young seals, but not pups, are with their parents in September and October immediately north of the Worm. There are fewer in winter and when it is rough.

Dolphins arrive in late May and stay until August or early September, following the fish. These are the short-beaked common dolphins, which will play around recreational craft and give visitors a treat. Bottle-nosed dolphins are at New Quay in Ceredigion, but are not seen off Gower, although Risso's dolphins may rarely be sighted from the boat. Minkie, hump-backed and pilot whales are as exciting as they are rare. Sea Watch Foundation at New Quay is given details of Gower sightings. Harbour porpoise are seen off headlands: Pwlldu, Oxwich, Port Eynon and Worms Head. They roll through the surface of the water and very seldom jump clear. They are best seen in flat calm conditions and can be in numbers; but they do not interact with boats and do not engage with visitors in the way that dolphins do.

Not strictly a dedicated marine mammal, the European otter has made a dramatic comeback in the UK in recent years. Reduction in pesticide use and cessation of hunting has seen their return to most fresh waterways, including those, like Broad Pool and Oxwich South Pond, in Gower. However, as on the west coast of Scotland, otters have now also made their home near to the sea, adopting sea fish as their preferred diet. They have been seen in the sea at Oxwich, Three Cliffs Bay, Port Eynon, Fall Bay and Kitchen Corner near Worms Head. There is now every reason to include them in this list of sea mammals.

Gareth B. Thomas

Pwlldu Bay

FISH

High tide at Penclawdd

The seas around the Gower coast are home to a wide variety of species of fish. Some of these are targeted by commercial fishermen and will end up on the slabs at Swansea market, where a visitor may survey the rich suite of species landed, some familiar, such as mackerel, cod, bass, plaice, Dover and sand soles, turbot, grey mullet and coalfish (coley), and others more unfamiliar – red, grey and tub gurnards, ling, angler-fish (aka monkfish), skates, conger eels, dabs and flounders, and more recently grey triggerfish, to name a few.

Local fishermen and angling visitors may be fortunate to secure some of these from rock and beach fishing marks. The recent global sea temperature rise has brought the exotic triggerfish to Gower waters, particularly the Mumbles area. More frequently however they may capture some other common species, not normally recognised for their culinary merit, but providing the sport that shore anglers seek without necessarily fishing 'for the pot'. These would include pollack, a handsome copper-hued relative of the cod and coalfish (distinct from the ubiquitous commercial pollock from the Pacific) which sadly has little culinary value, whiting, bib and pouting, with similar attributes, and a range of small sharks: lesser and greater spotted dogfish, common and starry smooth-hounds and tope. Mackerel fishermen may well be pestered by garfish, an eel-like swordfish, and horse mackerel – particularly in fading light.

The use of a small fishing boat will give access to a different variety of species, often found in off-shore wrecks: congers, ling, pollack and tope are targets. But the boat also offers the chance to see other large fish near the surface which may not be easily visible from the shore. Here we may find a basking shark, ocean sunfish, and blue and mako sharks following the mackerel shoals close in.

Finally, along the tide's edge on the shoreline at low tide, the local sand residents may briefly appear: greater and lesser sandeels, Boyer's sand-smelt and weever-fish all frequent this tidal zone. There is always the chance of coming across a dead specimen of any of the above species, from natural causes to trawling casualties, and possibly the only chance to witness the remarkable greater pipefish, seen from time to time.

Gareth B. Thomas

Mumbles Lighthouse

INVERTEBRATES

Strandline beetle Gareth B Thomas

The varied geology, rich diversity of habitats and mild oceanic climate are key attributes that make Gower a rich hunting ground for those who study invertebrates. The south-facing limestone cliffs and sand dunes are perhaps the most well-known habitats as they host a large number of nationally rare and scarce species as well as an abundance of commoner species. The cliffs and slopes at Overton are a good place to sample this richness, where species such as the Red Data Book moth the silky wave *Idaea dilutaria* can be disturbed in high summer, the larvae later feeding on the abundant common rock-rose *Helianthemum nummularium* that grows there. Other rarities occurring here include dotted bee-fly *Bombylius discolor*, large scabious mining-bee *Andrena hattorfiana* and blunthorn nomad cuckoo-bee *Nomada flavopicta*, all of which are soft-cliff inhabitants with fascinating and intricate life histories. More frequently-encountered species include the glow-worm *Lampyris noctiluca*, with the bioluminescent females being easy to spot after dark along many sections of cliff path. Among the species frequently encountered by those walking the coastal path during spring time are two large black beetles: the bloody-nosed beetle *Timarcha tenebricosa* which exudes bright red fluid from its mouth when threatened and whose unique larva may be found on its host plant, lady's bedstraw

Galium verum – and the black oil beetle *Meloe proscarabaeus*, the females of which have enormously enlarged abdomens that extend well beyond the wing capsules. In late summer and autumn the song of the predatory great green bush-cricket *Tettigonia viridissima*, the UK's largest insect, can be heard from hedgerows and scrub all along the coast, but spotting one of these great ventriloquists is more of a challenge.

During daylight hours the careful observer of moths might also find the larvae of samphire knot-horn *(Epischnia asteris)*, cliff plume *Agdistis meridionalis* and chestnut-coloured carpet *Thera cognata* on their respective host plants, namely golden samphire *Inula crithmoides*, rock sea-lavender *Limonium binervosum* and juniper *Juniperus communis*.

Marbled white

Sand dunes support an equally varied and important assemblage of species, a prime example being the strandline beetle *Eurynebria complanata*, now only known in the UK from three beaches around Carmarthen Bay, including Whiteford Sands. Other attractive scarce species include the pied winged robberfly *Pamponerus germanicus* and the dung beetle *Onthophagus nuchicornis*, which is reliant here on the dung of Gower's ponies. Whiteford is the best place in Gower to find the minuscule narrow-mouthed whorl snail *Vertigo angustior*, which lives along a seepage line between the dunes and saltmarsh. The Gower money spider *Baryphyma gowerense*, first discovered at Whiteford in 1964, is the only species named after the peninsula; its principal habitat is upper saltmarsh with stands of sea rush *Juncus maritimus.*

Away from the Burry Inlet the other significant wetland habitats are the extensive marshy grasslands found on commons and in rough pastures. The invertebrate assemblage associated with these habitats is of particular importance, with headline species such as the marsh fritillary *(Euphydryas aurinia)* and narrow-bordered bee hawk *Hemaris tityus*, the larvae of both feeding on the foliage of devil's-bit scabious *Succisa pratensis*. The complex of runnels on Cefn Bryn support the nationally scarce southern damselfly *Coenagrion mercuriale*, with the adjacent mosaic of bog and heath supporting a wealth of invertebrate species; these include large and colourful species such as emperor moth *Saturnia pavonia* and emperor dragonfly *Anax imperator*, such sights invariably complemented by a background chorus of foraging bees and courting grasshoppers.

Other Gower habitats well worth exploring, each of which has its own characteristic suite of species, include the fens and marshes at Oxwich and Llanrhidian, the heathland and mire mosaics of the Gower commons, examples of which can be found from Rhossili up on to Mynydd y Gwair, the Gower ash woods and the upland sessile oak woods, not forgetting areas of parkland and even gardens, which support a surprising abundance of invertebrate species; for example, over 700 species of moth alone have been recorded in a typical urban garden in Gorseinon.

The species and habitats mentioned here hopefully provide a taster of what Gower has to offer and, whether you are a casual observer or passionate entomologist, the wealth of invertebrates that can be found is truly remarkable. However, be prepared to take time and look carefully. The more time and care you take, the more you will see and the more you will be amazed.

Barry Stewart

Green Hairstreak

BIRDS

Skylark

The visitor is likely to be here in spring or summer, so let's start with some spring migrants.

Cuckoos should be in their preferred places and calling by the third week of April. In Wales, unlike the Scottish west coast and Hebrides, the cuckoo is in retreat. Try Cwm Ivy Marsh and Llanmadoc. The western flank of Ryers Down is good habitat but not fruitful these last few years. Oxwich ought to be good, as should Llangennith Burrows. In inland Gower you might hear three or four between the Lliw Valley reservoirs on a calm day in May. There, too, are wheatears, red kites, stonechats, redstarts, redpolls, stock doves and – if very lucky – a whinchat. Kites are now breeding in the north of the peninsula, but their stronghold is inland Gower and particularly Mynydd y Gwair and the hills.

Wood warblers and pied flycatchers are in oakwood cwms only in inland Gower. Pied flycatchers are intensively studied at Cwm Clydach. Whitethroat and lesser whitethroat are found throughout, the former breeding in good numbers on the cliffs and Cwm Ivy Marsh. Spotted flycatchers are now a rarity in the peninsula and should be reported to the Gower Ornithological Society. Some blackcaps over-winter here; in spring the returning males are to be heard very widely. Reed and sedge warblers are at Oxwich.

Dartford warblers breed in Gower, but skulk. The south coast is best, anywhere from Limeslade to the Coastwatch at Rhossili.

Gower Ringing Group is active, chiefly at Oxwich National Nature Reserve. South Pond, seen from the public hide, is not as good as it was. Cetti's warblers and water rails will be heard. A pair of mute swans breeds. Up to half a dozen little grebes are present and some breed. There are moorhens, but for reasons unexplained, coot no longer.

In late August or September scanning north from Wernffrwd with a telescope might reward you with an osprey. (As a spring passage migrant they are scarcer.) In winter Wernffrwd and Llanrhidian are home to hen harriers and short-eared owls.

Green woodpeckers are widely heard, often on the grassland above Gower's cliffs or at Llanmadoc and Betty Church Wood. Great spotted woodpeckers are common but shy. Lesser spotted woodpecker is breeding in our area, but the location is not being made known.

Chough

Anywhere on the south coast or at Rhossili, look out for those aristocrats amongst crows, the choughs. Their red legs and bills are distinctive. They are back in Gower as if they had never been away. The call is in a higher register than the jackdaws' with which they are often seen, and it is the call which usually brings them to notice. Hunts Farm, Three Cliffs National Trust carpark and Pobbles are good places to look; also Mewslade, Devil's Truck and Rhossili.

Fulmars are on the cliffs as breeding birds and are present but scarce in winter. Fall Bay and Lewes Castle are good, or try Spaniard Rocks and the nameless tidal beach north-east of Burry Holms. Pied wagtails are common, seemingly more so when you know their flight call. Expect to see them on roofs and pavements (where food must surely be in short supply) or on the strand line at Port Eynon, picking up sand hoppers. Occasionally they are in flocks. Grey wagtails and dippers are on the small streams in the peninsula but in better numbers inland.

Waders are chiefly on the north Gower salt marsh, on the shore of the Burry Inlet and at Blackpill. Winter, of course, is best. A long circular walk from Cwm Ivy carpark to Whiteford Point and back is rewarding. Whilst redshanks can always be seen at a great distance, satisfactory views are had, save at high tide, from Dalton's Point and the carpark in central Penclawdd. Dalton's Point is also excellent for black-tailed godwit, an attractive species unexpectedly gaining ground strongly. Purple sandpipers might be seen under Mumbles Pier, at Sedgers' Bank at Port Eynon or on the Crabart. They are attractive and confiding waders, not doing as well as they once did. Whimbrel are passage migrants. Curlew are chiefly in the Burry Inlet, but a few might be heard on the rocks near Pwlldu or Hunts Bay.

Wildfowl include eiders. They have been at the north-west of the peninsula for many years but do not breed. (As they are not immortal, we have to suppose that breeding birds go north.) A large winter population of scoters is on Carmarthen Bay, diving to feed on mussels at the bottom. (Recording year 2014: 'max 6000' in late January.) Ideally, aerial photographic counting is needed. In the Burry Inlet there is an important winter population of pintail; there are wigeon, teal and shelduck. Wildfowlers have rights over some part of the marsh; a grazier with conflicting rights has to parley an accommodation with them.

At the turn of the year, over 400 great crested grebes, widely spread out, might be counted in Swansea Bay between the River Neath and Mumbles Pier.

Raptors include kestrels in small numbers, breeding. The cliffs and Llanrhidian are likely spots to see them. When they fly down and pounce, it might be on beetles or bush crickets. Sparrowhawks are plentiful; the males take small garden and woodland birds, and the females bigger prey. Visitors are less likely to see them than are the owners of a garden with well-stocked feeders. Goshawks (a re-introduced species) are in Penllergaer Valley Woods and sometimes the peninsula. Such devastating killers are they, that they might make the journey from valued rarity to pest in not many years. Buzzards are seen above woods and commons, their numbers somewhat down. It should be remembered that buzzard is a woodland species: you might surprise one in Millwood or Clyne and see it getting away under the canopy, its flight laboured but quiet.

Grey Heron

Grey herons are in decline for reasons not fully known. Little and great white egrets are increasing. The Wildlife and Wetlands Trust centre at Penclacwydd attracts rarities amongst the herons and owls. Unsurprisingly, birds first seen there are often seen in Gower too. Bittern are only occasionally here, generally in winter; but their status can change quite quickly.

Unusual birds in Gower? You might be lucky and see a merlin on the salt marsh or Whiteford dune slacks. There are Slavonian grebes off Whiteford Point in winter; also mergansers and great northern divers. Red- and black-throated divers might be seen off the

Causeway, Rhossili. Lapwing has almost disappeared as a breeding bird but survives as a numerous and welcome winter visitor. Golden plover are in hundreds in winter – thousands a short distance away in estuarine Carmarthenshire.

Sea watching is a minority interest amongst birdwatchers. Surprises turn up off Bracelet Bay and Port Eynon Point: gannets, shearwaters, auks, skuas and even storm petrels.

Crossbill sightings are generally in forestry in inland Gower. In the peninsula try the plantation on Whiteford sandspit. Recent records there have been in February August and September. The common tits remain common, chiefly in woodland and at garden feeders. An exception, here, must be made for marsh tits, which are in decline, and their congener the willow tit, which is now a considerable rarity.

Winter thrushes, the fieldfares and redwings, are most commonly seen in a hard winter, when they may be driven into gardens for food. Blackbirds should be recognised as a partial migrant, with numbers increasing greatly in winter. If seen at all, ring ouzels might be on high ground in inland Gower in April or May; and in 2013 (a particularly good year) were at several locations in the peninsula during the spring migration.

Our last hard winter almost wiped out Gower's attractive stonechats. As partial migrants they were expected to recover quickly and they did. However, six or eight years on, they are not the common breeding bird they used to be between Limeslade and Langland.

Kingfishers are a favourite but scarce in our area. You might be lucky when walking along Clyne Stream or Burry Stream in the peninsula; or beside slow fresh water rivers and streams in inland Gower. Nests are not advertised and are protected by law. The rule of thumb is that there is no right of way along the banks of rivers or streams.

Linnets are common, winter and summer. Along with goldfinches (also common) they benefit from The National Trust's important initiatives on The Vile in Rhossili. Yellowhammers might benefit in Rhossili too, but at present their numbers are markedly down and their attractive spring song is heard infrequently – on the cliffs and on farmland.

The City Council and the proprietor of Mumbles Pier are working to keep up kittiwake numbers at their breeding colony there. The unproven theory is that peregrines drove kittiwakes away from their old home at Devil's Truck.

Gower's emblematic bird? The handsome and strident oystercatcher.

Peter Douglas-Jones

Oystercatcher: Gower's emblematic bird

OTHER ANIMAL LIFE

Ponies on Ryer's Down

Gower's rich variety of habitats supports a range of creatures. Within this small area can be found a rare combination of coastal, upland and marine environments: woodland, limestone grassland, sand dunes, fresh-water marsh and salt-water marsh, reed beds, cliffs, farmland, heaths.

Invertebrates flourish here supporting a range of other animals. The bird population is covered in another chapter, but there are bats – the rare greater and lesser horseshoe bats, noctule, Natterer's, Daubenton's, whiskered, and common and soprano pipistrelle and brown long-eared are all known to be here. They benefit from the cliff caves and woodland with ponds where they can find safe roosts and plenty of food to rear their young as at Killay Marsh or Cwm Ivy Marsh. They are closely monitored. Bat populations are doing well nationally but some varieties such as Serotine's and the brown long-eared found in Gower are becoming rare. Daubenton's are found at a few sites in Gower generally near water. Roost sites can be lost when farm buildings are upgraded for new uses – there is a record from over fifteen years ago of 100 bats being found in a cavity wall.

Water is important – the coastal area has its own environment. The ponds on Gower provide essential water for the domestic animals found on the commons such as cattle, ponies and sheep. Broad Pool at Cillibion is the largest pool with an area of 0.81 hectares. It has been there since at least 1645 and has rarely dried out. Sticklebacks can be found there and a variety of invertebrates. In December 2017 there were reports of a large dog otter fishing at Broad Pool mid-morning undisturbed by the traffic alongside. The numerous streams have also benefited the recovering otter population; a few individuals have been identified by DNA from spraints on a four km stretch of the Clyne river. Otters have been seen on the beach at Three Cliffs bay, at South Pond, Oxwich (reports of sightings are put up in the public hide at Oxwich) and on the cameras tracking areas of NT land at Cwm Ivy Marsh. They do well in both freshwater areas and on the coast, enjoying fishing rock pools exposed at low tide. Birds form an important part of their diet. They are also found in upland Gower around the Lliw river. Otters were hunted until the 1920s and this, together with the effect of pesticides, contributed to their decline right up to the 1970s.

Other mustelids found locally include badgers, weasels, polecats and polecat ferrets, mink and stoats. Pine marten were last seen in Gower in the late 1980s. Stoats and weasels like open grassland and weasels have been seen hunting for voles or rabbits along the boundary walls near Longhole Cave, Overton. A mink was reported on the river Loughor in June 2018 on the Carmarthenshire bank. Animals such as rabbits and voles provide for owls and other hunting birds as well as for the healthy fox population (rural and urban). Badgers are seen but many are found with TB. Hedgehogs are declining here as well as nationally. Other small rodents include wood mice and pygmy shrews which have been known to use the blue tit and great tit nesting boxes in the Berry Wood Reserve. There are also some native hazel-dormice populations.

Hares are seen but not as commonly as formerly, usually on open land like Fairwood Common. Rabbits are in a poor state, suffering from myxomatosis and rabbit viral haemorrhagic disease. Some local ecosystems such as the Oxwich dunes are becoming grassed over without rabbits to graze them and grasslands also depend on them to keep scrub at bay. The buzzard numbers may be down because of fewer rabbits.

Local reptiles include grass snakes and adders though there

is debate as to which is more common. Adders are shy and not aggressive unless interfered with and are more dangerous to dogs than their owners, lying hidden in the grass. It's worth checking the ground before putting down your picnic rug! Slow-worms are around but decreasing. Common lizards are seen as well. Palmate newts, common toads and frogs are to be found but they are affected by the loss of local ponds and pools. Such pools can also be home to sticklebacks, eels, trout and bay flounders as well as many invertebrates.

Several organisations overlap in the care, management and ownership of Gower. Natural Resources Wales manages the environment and natural resources on behalf of the Welsh Assembly. Swansea Council has responsibility for many parks, woodlands and natural areas. National Trust owns substantial areas, the Wildlife Trust of South and West Wales manages over twenty nature reserves. There are Local Nature Reserves, as at Broad Pool, Cillibion, and four National Nature Reserves – Oxwich, Whiteford, Gower Coast and Pant y Sais, and many SSSIs from Mawr/Swansea uplands to Rhossili both of which are also Sites of Importance for Nature Conservation.

Gower is very rich in its ecosystems but it is also fragile and vulnerable to overuse. Many people and organisations are involved in protecting and studying the environment here. As visitors and residents we too need to show our appreciation of this remarkable area by our care for it.

Jane Sherrard-Smith

Cattle on Pennard East Cliff common

Rabbit in brambles

THE RURAL ECONOMY

Taking in the view, Rhossili Beach

Historically, the predominant land use in the peninsula and upland Gower was farming. The south and west of the peninsula attracted the acquisitive Normans, and there the Welsh were swept aside. They had to make do with the poorer farming land of the north and east of the peninsula and with the valleys and bare hills north of Swansea. An ever fainter linguistic divide remains today along a line between Gower's two lighthouses, Whiteford and Mumbles. The same line roughly demarcates the coalfield. Within living memory there have been mining and heavy industry in north-east peninsular Gower and along the valleys of the rivers Loughor, Amman, Twrch and Tawe.

The City and County of Swansea is not quite co-extensive with the old lordship of Gower. Current employment figures 'by broad industry group' show that agriculture, forestry and fishing together account for only 0.2% of the working population. That startling figure should be borne in mind when reading about farming below. Manufacturing is 5.5%, which should worry those of us who think this country must make things. Construction is also 5.5%. Education (universities and all schools) is 9.1% and health, the biggest category by far, 17.3%. The population of Wales's second city is just under 250,000 and therefore extensive urbanisation has affected employment both in rural and urban Swansea.

The peninsula visibly supports farming, tourism and leisure. Mixed farming was the rule. After WWII, the Penrice Estate sold most of its tenanted farms. As a result, most of the farms in the peninsula are freehold, of an average of 120 acres, owned and farmed by the descendants of the tenants of those days.

Sheep farming on Gower

The demise of mixed farming, a country-wide trend, will probably lead to a more specialised approach of managing land – a challenge to Gower's farmers. The production of commodities such as cauliflowers and potatoes is hugely diminished. Dairying, too, has shrunk to just a few farms. Beef cattle remain, often with a considered and valid business model, but sometimes with a farmer running mixed breeds of cattle on the inland commons, cliff tops, village greens and verges. Gower's commons are a distinctive feature, both of the landscape and of minority farming methods. However, in north Gower, sheep farming is important. The vast salt marshes of the Burry Estuary have traditionally made good grazing for sheep, and farms in that proximity have sensibly utilised that unusual characteristic and marketed the lamb successfully as 'saltmarsh'.

The north Gower marshes have traditionally been the home of the cockle industry, centred in Penclawdd, Crofty and Wernffrwd. Until relatively recent times (late 1900s) cockles have been gathered by hand in conditions of considerable hardship. In later years, some of this has been mechanised (the donkeys and carts relegated to the past) but it can still be hard and backbreaking work. Recent difficulties with the health of the cockle beds have vastly diminished their productivity and a question mark hangs over their future.

As we proceed through the 21st century, the land is being adapted to accommodate new economic and ecological demands. In north Gower for example, around Three Crosses, there has sprung up a thriving business based on growing Christmas trees on the acid soils of that area. Since its inception in 1997 the business has grown to be the largest producer of Christmas trees in Wales. Currently, there are 260 acres under cultivation and sales stand at around 400,000 trees per year. To assist sales, a small herd of reindeer is also maintained. Since the 1960s there has been a poultry farm at Kittle, and with expansion in the 1990s now has upwards of 400,000 birds producing eggs.

Farms, as well as catering businesses, have developed wedding venues in the peninsula that have made Gower one of the most desirable places in the country in which to get married. The contribution of the wedding business to the local economy is significant both in employment and financially.

Wind farm, Mynydd y Gwair

Within peninsular Gower there have been a few spaces utilised for electricity generation from solar panels – these have had little or no impact on the landscape, unlike the wind farms generating power in Mawr. The 16 turbines on Mynydd y Gwair should generate 32.8MW of power (enough for 22,000 homes) but at considerable cost to the precious wild landscape so close to Swansea. The projected wind farm around Lundy Island met with vigorous opposition from the AONB and National Parks adjacent and was not developed.

The leisure/holiday business in Gower now makes a major contribution to the local economy and also has a significant impact on the landscape. The land use which announces itself visually is caravans, touring and static. It may be that planning consents were granted too easily in past decades but Swansea Council takes a keen interest in these caravan and camping sites. Self-catering properties have also been developed, usually by way of conversion from byres and outbuildings.

Shops, depending largely on the tourist industry, thrive during the summer months. Those with 'Surf' on their fascias are also numerous but leisure activities also include sky-diving, pony trekking, walking, birdwatching, sea angling, cycling, swimming, sailing and coastal cruises in small RIBs. The peninsula, the aerodrome and the nearby marina lend themselves to these activities.

The Gower peninsula has changed dramatically in recent decades with the increasing dependence on tourism. But, equally important, is the growth of Swansea with its need for housing. Villages are becoming dormitories for the city and are steadily expanding to accommodate this need. At the same time, many village houses are becoming desirable acquisitions in the second-home market – this, too, presents challenges to the local economy. We seem to be living in a period of pivotal change when many of the assertions of this article and even this guide are less secure than they were a few decades ago. The section on 'Conservation' in this guide needs to be read as a vital corollary to 'The Rural Economy'.

Peter Douglas-Jones

CONSERVATION AND GOWER

Mewslade wall Rhossili

Global issues – such as the proper management of resources, reducing pollution and conserving what is best for the future – affect us all; but this short article concentrates on the immediate and local needs of conservation in Gower.

Gower is a happy accident of geological forces, climatic conditions and human enterprise: a harmonious blend of landscape, nature and history. This '*rare patch of the Earth's surface*', as Wynford Vaughan Thomas called it, is a rich mix of natural scenic beauty, farmed landscape and diverse flora. Much of Gower had remained unspoilt, not through a positive intention to conserve it but because of the traditionalism of the large estates. The mid-20th century break-up of the estates (largely because of crippling inheritance tax), coinciding with the huge increase in car ownership, largely ended this safeguard. The protection of natural isolation had gone for ever. Suddenly Gower's vulnerability was exposed, and exploitation became a serious and urgent reality. With no railway and poor roads, tourism hardly existed in Gower until after WWII.

The Gower Society had been established early in 1948, mainly to study Gower and to produce a journal of its findings. Within a few months, however, the role of conservationist was thrust upon it when plans were announced for a Butlin's-type holiday camp at

Rhossili. The campaign to prevent the '*despoliation of this untouched tip of Gower*' was so successful that the Society became the natural leader in campaigns over the next few years to prevent the destruction of Oxwich Castle keep, the felling of Crawley Woods and the establishment of a shell-testing range in the Burry Estuary.

While tourism has undoubtedly brought benefits to Gower, it has also brought great challenges. On a fine summer's day 50,000 day visitors will join the 30,000 holiday makers enjoying an environment that they might be helping to destroy. While we delight in sharing Gower with those who enjoy our beaches, cliffs and countryside and those who appreciate beauty, peace and tranquillity, there is a danger from too many feet, too many wheels and too many hooves. The increased crowdedness, the litter, the worn-down look are familiar signs of excessive human pressure. The fundamental question is, as Goodman asked in the first edition of this Guide, whether we are skilful enough in managing our environment to balance the many purposes of Gower without subjecting it to pressures it cannot sustain.

The designation, in 1956, of much of peninsular Gower as the first Area of Outstanding Natural Beauty (AONB) in the United Kingdom was widely welcomed. Jenkin John, Chairman of the County Planning Committee, announced that '*In Gower, private interest will take second place to public interest*'. But the designation was a two-edged sword: while it gave status to the area, it gave only minimal protection, and increased the pressures from both visitors and developers.

Gower is unique. In its mild climate and diverse habitat, upwards of one thousand species of plant flourish, including a dozen types of orchid and the yellow whitlow grass, a plant found in the wild nowhere else in Britain. The AONB comprises almost exactly half of the 38,000 hectares of the old lordship (and present-day City and County of Swansea). There are four National Nature Reserves, including the Ramsar site on the Burry Estuary, seventeen other nature reserves, twenty-seven Sites of Special Scientific Interest and fifty-five hectares of Heritage Coastline. Add to this the wealth of pre-historic remains, including one of the earliest human burials found in Britain, prehistoric art, cairns, Bronze Age dolmens and forts, together with a host of castles and churches, a fair sprinkling of domestic buildings – and the richness of Gower becomes apparent.

The delicate balance that produces such an abundance of life needs not only protection, but positive and sympathetic management. Management is essential. Left to themselves, buildings decay and fall into ruin; woodlands deteriorate, commons turn into scrublands. The south Gower limestone cliff land exemplifies the problems of management; in some parts towards the west, overgrazing by sheep has led in hot dry summers to scorched, almost bare, earth which, when the rain has returned, has been colonised by plantain rather than grass. To the east, increased human and dog populations have led to farmers withdrawing their sheep from the cliffs, with the result that some parts would now be almost impassable because of bramble, gorse and bracken were it not for the sterling work of National Trust and other voluntary agencies.

Management involves choices. Choices between what is to be protected and what is to be destroyed, what is to be encouraged and what discouraged. What principles direct our priorities? When only one domain is under consideration, the answer is relatively straightforward: we favour the rare rather than the commonplace, and variety above monotony. In a choice between the fen orchid and the dandelion, the fen orchid will always have priority. We clear bracken in the hope of halting its monocultural progress, and allowing the regeneration of the cowslips, bluebells and campions that have been choked out by the bracken's absolute domination of its habitat. The same principles of rarity and variety apply to archaeological and historical remains, but circumscribed by the knowledge that, once they are lost, such remains can never be resurrected.

The real problems arise when there is a conflict of priorities between one domain of interest and another; between rock-climbers and nesting kittiwakes, walkers and eroded footpaths, house builders and visual amenity. Compromise might be possible: the climbers can be allowed the cliffs for nine months, and the birds given priority for three; footpaths can be re-directed, if only temporarily, to allow recovery or sympathetic strengthening; a change of position or of construction material can change a house from being a blot on a beautiful landscape to an acceptable, even attractive part of the vista.

Sometimes the conflict is between the global and the local. In global terms wind turbines must be a 'good thing'. They produce power in a comparatively clean and renewable way. But, if in doing so, they destroy an area of wild beauty, an area of peace and tranquillity, an area of particular and special culture, where does the balance of profit and loss lie?

Final stone in the wall at Mewslade Gordon Howe

An AONB is a particularly attractive area in which to live, particularly when it is in easy reach of a centre of population. Consequently, it is a particularly profitable area in which to build houses. Far too many buildings have got through the planning net, and far too often money has not been matched by taste. New and replacement housing, if it is not to be damaging to the environment, needs to be strictly controlled in amount, location and design. It needs to meet a social or economic need of the community and make a positive contribution to the village scene. Need, not greed, must be the criterion. Other developments, be they tourist or commercial, must also be of a scale and type that recognises the sensitivity of the AONB. There is a real danger of creeping suburbanisation: overhead power and telephone cables, telecommunications masts, unnecessary kerbing of roads, a proliferation of large and badly-designed signs advertising 'attractions' – all these can subtly alter the experience of being in the countryside. And most of them are unnecessary.

The rural landscape of Gower owes a great deal to its combination of commons and small fields, some of medieval origin. Hedges, banks, ponds, copses and marshy hollows have survived as part of a traditional farmed landscape. Despite increased pressures on farmers, every effort should be made to retain these traditional features and to seek support for the farmers to enable them to do so. As Michael Haines has pointed out in The Gower Society Conference 1996, (AONBs: The Way Forward): *For the individual farmers, food and recreation are goods he can sell; but the public goods of landscape, wildlife habitat and quality of environment are a by-product for which he cannot charge*. If support for food subsidies declines, and with it the farmers' income, then the only way to maintain those public goods in sensitive areas such as AONBs might be a long-term environmental support system. Economic laws do not recognise AONB boundaries, and the greatest protection we can give to our landscape is to ensure a strong and viable local farming community.

Conservation is not about maintaining the *status quo*; still less about returning to some artificially idyllic, pre-industrial revolution dream. It is about managing change in a way that allows the essential character of Gower – its natural scenic beauty, its farmed landscape, its history and its diverse flora – to remain. We shall not go far wrong if we recognise the need to balance conservation with the legitimate well-being of the community, without allowing the short-term financial gain of the few to be attained at the long-term expense of the heritage that belongs to us all. If we remember that Gower was not given to us by our fathers, but lent to us by our children, we shall not let them, or it, down.

Malcolm Ridge

Three Cliffs

Rhossili Beach to Burry Holms

FURTHER READING

Many people have been inspired to write about Gower and there are some wonderful books to complement a visit. Some, like Nigel Jenkins's *Real Gower*, give a very personal view while others, like Jonathon Mullard's *Gower,* give an exceptional overview of a unique landscape. Sadly, these are now out-of-print, but we think them worth seeking out, either online or in second-hand bookshops.

The following list of books is brief but should provide a starting point for exploring this area. Similarly, the recommended websites are a small selection of those that we think will be useful and help you to discover more about this unique place. The broadest archive is probably to be found in the many publications of the Gower Society, including the 70 *Gower* journals, which cover every conceivable topic relating to the area. Many back issues are available from the Society itself as are their publications listed here, either via the Gower Society website, or in good bookshops. Items out of print may be consulted in local libraries or through the outstanding and very helpful West Glamorgan Archive Service.

BOOKS

GOWER SOCIETY PUBLICATIONS

Gower	The Society's annual journal
Ernest Morgan: Architect of Swansea	Richard Porch 2018
Hidden Histories of Swansea and Gower	Gary Gregor 2014
Gower in Focus	Harold Grenfell
Gower Walks	1999
The Butterflies of Gower	2000
Vernacular Gower	2003
Rhossili	2004
The Castles of Gower	2005
The Caves of Gower	2006
Swansea Bay - the Coastal Route	2007
The Churches and Chapels of Gower	2007
Edgar Evans of Gower	2008
The First Sixty Years of the Gower Society	2008

Gower Way Leaflets

PLUS many out-of-print publications available second-hand or in local libraries

GENERAL

George, G.T. (2008, 2015) *The Geology of South Wales* ISBN 13: 9780955937125 Geoserv Publishing

Jenkins, N. (2014) *Real Gower* ISBN 9781781722190 Seren Books

Mullard, J. (2006) *Gower* ISBN 9780007160679 Collins New Naturalist Library/Harper Collins

Oakley, J. (2010, 2015) *Seashore Safaris* ISBN 9781905582334 Graffeg

WEBSITES - A VERY BRIEF SELECTION

The Gower Society Membership, programme, publications and youth	**thegowersociety.org.uk**
City and County of Swansea (CCS) This gathers together a great deal of useful information, including nature reserves, beaches, public transport, events, walks, West Glamorgan Archive Service	**swansea.gov.uk**
West Glamorgan Archive Service	**swansea.gov.uk/ westglamorganarchives**
The National Trust	**nationaltrust.org.uk**
Cadw The Welsh Government's historic environment service	**cadw.gov.wales**
The Glamorgan-Gwent Archaeological Trust (GGAT)	**ggat.org.uk**
Royal Commission on the Ancient and Historical Monuments of Wales	**rcahmw.gov.uk/**
The Wildlife Trust of South and West Wales	**welshwildlife.org**
National Resources Wales	**naturalresources.wales**
Gower Commons	**gowercommons.org.uk**
Wales Coast Path	**walescoastpath.gov.uk**